THE STANLEY CUP

OLD TIME Hockey TRIVIA

DON WEEKES

GREYSTONE BOOKS

Douglas & McIntyre

VANCOUVER/TORONTO

For my researcher, Janet Torge, and her two sons, Riel and Sammy, neither of whom really appreciate the fact that mom now knows as much about hockey as they do.

Greystone Books
A division of Douglas & McIntyre Ltd.
1615 Venables Street
Vancouver, British Columbia V5L 2H1

Canadian Cataloguing in Publication Data

Weekes, Don.
   The Stanley Cup

   ISBN 1-55054-509-4

   1. Stanley Cup (Hockey)—Miscellanea. 2. National Hockey League—Miscellanea. 3. Hockey—Miscellanea. I. Title.
GV847.7.W43 1996   796.962648   C96-910232-1

Editing by Anne Rose and Kerry Banks
Cover and text design by Peter Cocking
Front cover photograph courtesy of the *Montreal Star*
Back cover photograph courtesy of the Richard Bak collection
Printed and bound in Canada by Best Book Manufacturers

Every reasonable care has been taken to trace the ownership of copyrighted visual material. Information that will enable the publishers to rectify any reference or credit is welcome.

The publisher gratefully acknowledges the assistance of the Canada Council and of the British Columbia Ministry of Tourism, Small Business and Culture.

Table of CONTENTS

Each spring for better than a century, a chosen handful of men live out a dream and carry on the legacy of playing for the Stanley Cup. For a brief moment, they cast all aside and focus on one goal. To become champions: the best in an ice game they've played since boyhood.

Although hockey has changed dramatically since the days it was played in dim, smoky arenas by men wearing striped sweaters and handlebar moustaches, what hasn't altered is the essence of winning; the pure thrill of success and peer recognition.

Nor have defeat and heartbreak come any easier over the years. Pride and sacrifice raise the stakes during the playoffs, penalizing the loser without compromise. Fate and circumstance. Lots of guts. No glory.

The Stanley Cup tradition rewards and punishes both the famous as well as the unknown. Champions such as Mark Messier of New York or Boston's Mel "Sudden Death" Hill; teams such as the colourful Dawson City Nuggets of 1905 and the underdog, over-the-hill Toronto Maple Leafs of 1967.

It is also about the oldest trophy competed for in North American professional sport. As the game has grown up, so has the Cup, both in importance and in size. Its history of champagne and parades has another side: of being dented, dunked, stolen, scorched and defaced in a wild series of misadventures.

In the following pages you'll meet the superstars and unsung heroes, as well as the legendary coaches, front office eccentrics and dynasty builders who guided them as they blazed a trail of playoff highlights and records. All, for a brief time, found glory through talent and dedication on the way to the Stanley Cup.

DON WEEKES
July 1, 1996

THE HOME OPENER

Throughout the regular season, NHL teams compete for first place to gain home-ice advantage in the playoffs. But how much difference does playing at home really make in the "second" season? Since 1917–18, first-place teams have won the Cup 43 times in 78 years. And how often have the home teams won all seven games in a final series? In only two Cup finals: in 1955 and 1965. But more on that later. In our opening chapter, you've got home-ice advantage in our first round of questions. Remember, all the questions have a logical answer, so pick the multiple-choice statement that best fits.   *(Answers are on page 7)*

1.1   Which NHL player has won the most Stanley Cups?
A. Gordie Howe
B. Henri Richard
C. Mark Messier
D. Guy Lafleur

1.2   Which team consistently engraved its mascot's (or stickboy's) name on the Stanley Cup?
A. The Toronto Maple Leafs
B. The old Ottawa Senators
C. The New York Rangers
D. The Philadelphia Flyers

1.3   What made the 1954 Stanley Cup presentation ceremonies a historic occasion?

A. Both teams shook hands *after* the Cup ceremonies
B. A newly designed Cup was presented for the first time
✔C. The Cup was presented to a female owner
D. There was no Stanley Cup present

1.4   What is the greatest number of different teams with which a player has won the Stanley Cup?
A. Two teams
B. Three teams
✔C. Four teams
D. Five teams

1.5   What is the record for most goals by an individual in a single NHL playoff game?
A. Four goals
✔B. Five goals
C. Six goals
D. Seven goals

1.6   What new hockey fashion did the New York Rangers introduce during the 1974 playoffs?
✔A. Sweaters with player names
B. Neck guards
C. Helmets with player numbers
D. Better flexing gloves

1.7   Since 1927, how many U.S.-born players have scored a Stanley Cup-winning goal?
A. None
B. One player
C. Two players
✔D. Three players

1.8   Which was the first team to have its name inscribed on the Stanley Cup?
A. The Montreal Wanderers
B. The Toronto Victorias
✔C. The Montreal AAA
D. The Ottawa Silver Seven

1.9 **During the 1982 playoff games at Vancouver's Pacific Coliseum, how did fans mimic the Canucks coach?**
A. Fans shook their fists at the referee
✓B. Fans waved white towels
C. Fans shouted, "Need glasses ref!?"
D. Fans stood on their seats, waving their arms

1.10 **How many Oiler players were members of all five championship clubs in Edmonton? (Name them.)**
A. Five players
B. Six players
✓C. Seven players
D. Eight players

1.11 **During one 1960 semifinals game between Toronto and Detroit, the Red Wings got some "extra help." What was it?**
✓A. Players used pure oxygen before hitting the ice
B. Jack Adams made a one-game coaching comeback
C. A sports psychologist sat on the bench
D. Three goalies were rotated during the game

1.12 **Which championship team has the most names engraved on the Stanley Cup?**
A. The 1974 Philadelphia Flyers
B. The 1989 Calgary Flames
✓C. The 1992 Pittsburgh Penguins
D. The 1995 New Jersey Devils

1.13 **How many overtime periods were played in the longest game in NHL history?**
A. Less than three OT periods
B. Between three and four OT periods
C. Between four and five OT periods
✓D. More than five OT periods

1.14 **What is the unofficial record for octopus throwing at Detroit's Joe Louis Arena during the playoffs?**
A. 14 octopi

B. 34 octopi
✔ C. 54 octopi
D. 74 octopi

1.15 **In what year was a video replay first used to determine a Stanley Cup playoff result?**
A. 1986
B. 1989
✔ C. 1992
D. 1995

1.16 **How many years passed between the 1925 Victoria Cougars' Stanley Cup triumph and the next time a western team won the trophy?**
A. 10–20 years
B. 20–30 years
C. 30–40 years
✔ D. More than 50 years

1.17 **How many overtime goals did Mel "Sudden Death" Hill score to earn his nickname during the 1939 playoffs?**
A. None
B. Two OT goals
✔ C. Three OT goals
D. Four OT goals

1.18 **How many times in NHL history have the home teams won all four home games in a final series?**
A. Never
✔ B. Twice
C. Four times
D. Eight times

1.19 **Who holds the record for most goals scored during the Stanley Cup playoffs?**
✔ A. Wayne Gretzky
B. Mark Messier
C. Rocket Richard
D. Jari Kurri

1.20 Besides the normal incentives, what inspired the Leafs when they came from behind three games to none to win the Cup in 1942?
A. A guaranteed trip to Florida
B. A practical joke on the opposition by captain Syl Apps
✓C. An emotional letter from a little girl
D. An inspirational sermon by the team's chaplain

1.21 How many players' names were later added to the original engraving of the 1994 New York Rangers on the Stanley Cup?
A. None
✓B. Two names
C. Three names
D. Four names

1.22 Between 1980 and 1990, the Islanders and the Oilers won how many Stanley Cups?
A. Seven of 11 Cups
B. Eight of 11 Cups
✓C. Nine of 11 Cups
D. 10 of 11 Cups

1.23 According to NHL rules, who on a championship team can receive a miniature Stanley Cup trophy?
A. Only the players
B. Only the players and coaches
C. Only those whose names are engraved on the Stanley Cup
✓D. Anyone in the team organization

1.24 Besides Scotty Bowman, who is the only other NHL bench boss to coach 200 games and record 100 wins in the playoffs?
A. Dick Irvin
✓B. Al Arbour
C. Mike Keenan
D. Toe Blake

THE HOME OPENER

1.1 **B. Henri Richard**

Richard won a record 11 Stanley Cups during his 20-year tenure with the Montreal Canadiens. His first five Cups came in his first five NHL seasons when the Canadiens went on a five-in-a-row championship spree from 1956 to 1960. Richard never played more than four consecutive seasons without winning the Cup. In 180 playoff games, he scored 49 goals and 129 points. Two of those goals were Cup winners: one in 1966 against Detroit, and another versus Chicago in 1971. The only other individual to equal Richard's 11 championships is his former coach, Toe Blake, who won three Cups as a player and eight as Montreal's bench boss between 1956 and 1968.

Most Stanley Cup Wins

Cups	Player	Team	Cup Years
11	Henri Richard	Montreal	1956–1973
10	Jean Béliveau	Montreal	1956–1971
10	Yvan Cournoyer	Montreal	1965–1979
9	Claude Provost	Montreal	1956–1969
8	Red Kelly	Detroit/Toronto	1950–1967
8	Jacques Lemaire	Montreal	1968–1979
8	Maurice Richard	Montreal	1944–1960

1.2 **A. The Toronto Maple Leafs**

What we call a stickboy today was originally known as a mascot—usually a youngster who wore the team uniform in the pre-game skate to bring the club luck. Whenever they won the Stanley Cup, the Leafs added their mascot's name to the team's roster. Family connections were key. Kerry Day's name was inscribed four times during the Hap Day coaching era: in 1945, 1947, 1948 and 1949. Conn Smythe used his pull to get Hugh Smythe's name on the Cup in 1942, and Richard Smythe's name on in 1967.

1.3 **C. The Cup was presented to a female owner**
Instead of the usual all-male gathering at centre ice for Cup presentations, the 1954 ceremonies at Detroit's Olympia featured Marguerite Norris, who received the Stanley Cup as Red Wing co-owner. Norris, upon the death of her father, James, became the NHL's first female executive and the first woman to have her name engraved on the Cup. It's an honour she shares with two other women: Sonia Scurfield, co-owner of the champion 1989 Calgary Flames, and Marie-Denise DeBartolo York, president of the 1991 Pittsburgh Penguins.

1.4 **C. Four teams**
He may not be a household name, but Jack Marshall's achievement, playing on four different Cup-winning teams, has never been topped. His first championship came in 1901 with the Winnipeg Victorias; then, in 1902 and 1903, as a member of the Montreal AAA; in 1907 and 1910, with the Montreal Wanderers; and his final touch to a sterling career, in 1914, as the Toronto Blueshirts' player/manager. Marshall played on six league championship teams and five Stanley Cup winners, and led all playoff goal scorers twice. He was inducted into the Hockey Hall of Fame in 1965.

1.5 **B. Five goals**
Five players share the record for most playoff goals in a single game. Darryl Sittler and Reggie Leach traded five-goal games during the 1976 Flyers–Maple Leafs series, tying earlier marks set by Rocket Richard and Newsy Lalonde. Mario Lemieux did it most recently. In each case, the scorer's team won the game on home ice.

Most Playoff Goals in One Game

Goals	Player	Final Score	Opposing Goalie	Year
5	Newsy Lalonde	Mtl 6 – Ott 3	Clint Benedict	1919
5	Maurice Richard	Mtl 5 – Tor 1	Paul Bibeault	1944
5	Darryl Sittler	Tor 8 – Phi 5	Bernie Parent	1976
5	Reggie Leach	Phi 6 – Bos 3	Gilles Gilbert	1976
5	Mario Lemieux	Pit 10 – Phi 7	Ron Hextall	1989

1.6   A. Sweaters with player names

Not unlike the game itself, sweaters have gone through their own evolution since organized hockey began. The first jerseys were woollen and knitted by local women. Team emblems and stripes were always standard decoration, but player numbers didn't appear until around 1912. Little changed until the switch from wool to polyester in the 1960s, and when, in the 1974 playoffs, the New York Rangers sported the first player names stitched across the jersey back. Teams immediately picked up on the practice, which was soon adopted as an NHL rule.

1.7   D. Three players

Only seven Stanley Cup-winning goals have been scored by players born outside Canada. Swedish-born Bob Nystrom of the Islanders (1980) and the Penguins' Ulf Samuelsson (1991) potted Cup winners, as did the Oilers' Jari Kurri (1987) of Finland and Colorado's Uwe Krupp (1996) of Germany. Three Americans have scored Cup winners. In 1938, the Blackhawks' Carl Voss of Chelsea, Massachusettes, recorded the Cup-winning goal for Chicago, a team with an unprecedented eight U.S.-born players (surpassed only by 1995's New Jersey Devils with 12 American players); in 1950, Pete Babando of Braeburn, Pennsylvania, scored the Stanley Cup winner in seventh-game overtime for Detroit; and in 1995, Roseau, Minnesota, native Neal Broten notched the Devils' Cup winner.

Montreal AAA of 1893: Hockey's first Stanley Cup champions.

1.8   C. The Montreal AAA

The Stanley Cup was first presented to the Montreal Amateur Athletic Association (AAA) after the team finished the 1893 season in first place with seven wins and one loss. At that time, the premier league, the Amateur Hockey Association of Canada (AHA), had five teams: one in Ottawa, one in Quebec City and three in Montreal (the AAA, the Crystals and the Victorias). Without any official playoff season, the Cup trustees decided that the AAA's record made them the "leading hockey team in Canada." Interestingly, the Stanley Cup, not yet a treasured trophy, was almost rejected by the Montreal players when it was presented to AAA executives instead of the team captain. The players wanted to ship the Cup back to Ottawa, but team officials intervened. They were unwilling to insult the Cup's donator, Lord Stanley, Canada's governor general at the time.

1.9 **B. Fans waved white towels**
Vancouver's playoff towel-waving craze took inspiration from game two of the 1982 Conference finals at Chicago Stadium. After referee Bob Myers disallowed a Canuck goal and called several Vancouver penalties, coach Roger Neilson stuck a white towel on a player's stick and began waving it in mock surrender. The entire bench got into it and the result cost the team $11,000 in fines. The Canucks returned home for game three to a towel-waving frenzy at the Coliseum. Vancouver won the series 4–1 but was swept four straight by the mighty Islanders in the finals.

1.10 **C. Seven players**
Oilers Glenn Anderson, Grant Fuhr, Randy Gregg, Charlie Huddy, Jari Kurri, Kevin Lowe and Mark Messier played on all five Edmonton championship teams between 1984 and 1990. Wayne Gretzky was traded after captaining the Oilers to Cup number four in 1988.

1.11 **A. Players used pure oxygen before hitting the ice**
Coaches carry an arsenal of tricks to motivate players; sometimes even the bizarre ones work. But strike the "wonders" of pure oxygen from that list. During the 1960 Detroit–Toronto semifinals, with the series deadlocked a game apiece, the Red Wings used pure oxygen to gain an edge in game three. Ahead 4–3 in the third, the strategy seemed to be working when Wings rookie Gerry Melnyk tied the score. But, after 43 minutes of extra time, Leaf great Frank Mahovlich notched the winner, blowing the air (so to speak) out of the oxygen theory. Afterwards, Toronto coach Punch Imlach dismissed it as "a gimmick." Imlach should know. He had his own motivational scheme. Early in the series, Imlach had piled $1,250 worth of bills in the dressing room and scrawled on the

blackboard: "Take a good look at the centre of the floor. This represents the difference between winning and losing." Imlach's Leafs won the series in six.

1.12 C. The 1992 Pittsburgh Penguins

The Penguins submitted 52 names for engraving on the Cup in 1992. Along with players and bench coaches, they included the team president, owners, executives, trainers, equipment manager, conditioning coach and scouts. The list proved a real challenge to engravers who can allot only 12 square inches of Cup space per championship team. The solution? Each name was inscribed smaller than normal to make them all fit.

1.13 D. More than five OT periods

Game one of the 1936 Detroit Red Wings–Montreal Maroons semifinals was a test of endurance and enthusiasm for player and fan alike. A capacity crowd of 9,000 fans jammed the Montreal Forum through three scoreless periods. Then, the real marathon began. Five extra periods and 16:30 of play later, only a few thousand die-hards remained to witness Detroit's Mud Bruneteau score the winner on Lorne Chabot. The Montreal goalie faced 67 shots (the 67th being Bruneteau's goal), while his counterpart, the Wings' Norm Smith, survived the rain of rubber and earned the shutout, handling an astounding 90 shots! The game took almost six hours to complete.

The Longest Overtime Playoff Games

Time	Year	Final Score	Scorer
116:30	1936	Detroit 1 – Montreal Maroons 0	Mud Bruneteau
104:46	1933	Toronto 1 – Boston 0	Ken Doraty
79:15	1996	Pittsburgh 3 – Washington 2	Petr Nedved
70:18	1943	Toronto 3 – Detroit 2	Jack McLean
68:52	1930	Montreal 2 – NY Rangers 1	Gus Rivers
68:47	1987	NY Islanders 3 – Washington 2	Pat LaFontaine

1.14 **C. 54 octopi**

According to Al Sobotka, the Joe Louis Arena manager
who leads the clean-up crews, an unofficial record of 54
octopi were thrown during one game of the 1995 Stanley
Cup final series between the Red Wings and New Jersey
Devils. The playoff tradition dates back to the days of the
old Detroit Olympia in 1952, when Wings fans Jerry and
Pete Cusimano pitched the first octopus from the stands
as a "good-luck charm." In those days, teams played two
playoff rounds and could win the Cup in eight games.
After sweeping Toronto 4–0 in the first round and leading
Montreal 3–0 in the 1952 final series, the Cusimano
brothers figured the eight-tentacled sea creature was a
natural symbol for eight straight wins. Detroit won the
1952 Stanley Cup in eight, and today fans still toss an
average of about 25 octopi per game.

1.15 **C. 1992**

Detroit's Divisional semifinal victory over Minnesota was
a climb to the summit the hard way. Down 3–1 in games,
the Wings pulled off a 3–0 win in game five but found
themselves tied 0–0 after regulation time in game six. In
overtime, Detroit's Sergei Fedorov took a slap shot that
appeared to hit the Minnesota crossbar. After video official
Wally Harris examined the video replay, he signalled to
referee Rob Shick that the puck had indeed entered the
net. The Wings tied the series on Fedorov's overtime goal
and beat the North Stars in game seven for the series win.

1.16 **D. More than 50 years**

Before 1926, when the NHL assumed ownership of the
Stanley Cup, the Cup was a challenge trophy awarded in a
playoff series between the champions of Canada's eastern
and western leagues. Although the Pacific Coast Hockey
Association (PCHA) can be credited with expanding the
interest and talent in hockey during its brief 15-year
existence, it could do little to compete with the NHL once
expansion into the United States raised the stakes and
secured the best players during the 1920s. Attendance

Mel "Sudden Death" Hill: The unlikely overtime hero of 1939's Stanley Cup-winning Boston Bruins.

in the west fell and soon its two leagues collapsed, ending the annual east-west Cup challenge and any further hopes of a western Cup winner. After the Victoria Cougars' Cup victory in 1925, the west waited more than a half-century for another Stanley Cup champion. The long-overdue return of Lord Stanley's mug came in 1984 when the Edmonton Oilers defeated the New York Islanders.

1.17   **C. Three OT goals**
Boston's Mel Hill became an overnight sensation during the 1939 semifinals, when he scored an amazing three overtime goals in a classic, old-time Bruins–Rangers match-up. The seesaw series went into overtime four times, including a seventh-game nail-biter that required 48 minutes of extra play before Hill wired the series winner. Hill, in his rookie playoff year, became "Sudden Death" and found instant celebrity status in Boston. Ironically, Rangers manager Lester Patrick had turned down Hill years earlier because he was "too frail for big-time hockey." Today, Hill stands alone in the NHL record books with the most overtime goals in one playoff series.

1.18   **B. Twice**
Since the seven-game format began in 1939, only two Cup finals, the 1955 and the 1965 series, have gone the full distance with the home team winning each of its games. In 1955, Detroit had home-ice advantage against Montreal and took the final series 4–3, as both teams won all their home games. And in 1965, Montreal with home advantage, defeated Chicago 4–3, as both clubs won all their home games. Meanwhile, there has never been a final series in which the home teams lost all seven games.

1.19   **A. Wayne Gretzky**
As of 1996, the Great One holds NHL records for most playoff goals (112), most assists (250) and most points (362). Although Jari Kurri and Mark Messier are right behind him in goals, both have a long way to go to equal his record of total points.

Playoff Goal-Scoring Leaders*

Player	Teams	Years	GP	G	A	PTS
Wayne Gretzky	Edm/LA/St L	15	193	**112**	250	362
Mark Messier	Edm/NYR	16	221	**106**	177	283
Jari Kurri	Edm/LA/NYR	13	185	**105**	125	230
Glenn Anderson	Edm/Tor/NYR/St L	15	225	**93**	121	214
Mike Bossy	New York Islanders	10	129	**85**	75	160
Maurice Richard	Montreal	15	133	**82**	44	126
Jean Béliveau	Montreal	17	162	**79**	97	176

* Totals current to 1996.

1.20　**C. An emotional letter from a little girl**

It's not the kind of sentimentality that would motivate players in today's game, but when coach Hap Day marched into the Maple Leafs' dressing room prior to game four with a letter from a distraught young female fan, it was just the inspiration needed to shake up his 0–3 team. The little girl said she would be ashamed to go to school the next day if Toronto lost the Cup in four straight. After Day's speech, Leafs forward Sweeney Schriner spoke up: "Don't worry about this one Skipper. We'll win it for the little girl!" And they did: One victory after another, steamrolling the favoured Wings with four in a row. The Leafs' miraculous comeback of '42 is the only championship ever won by a team that trailed 0–3 in a Cup finals.

1.21　**B. Two names**

New York raised a big stink after Rangers Eddie Olczyk and Mike Hartman were left off the Stanley Cup in 1994. Both players failed to qualify (a minimum of 42 regular-season games or finals action was required) as champions under NHL rules, yet Olczyk and Hartman attended all practices and travelled with the team. Under pressure, the NHL relented and the names E. Olczyk and M. Hartman were stamped alongside their Cup-winning teammates.

Syl Apps: Toronto captain of three Stanley Cup championships, including the come-from-behind miracle series of 1942.

1.22 **C. Nine of 11 Cups**

The decade-long domination of the Islanders and Oilers can only be compared to the stranglehold Montreal and Toronto had on the Cup when they won 13 of 14 Cups between 1956 and 1969. The Islanders captured the Cup four years in a row between 1980 and 1983; then Edmonton took five Cups in seven seasons from 1984 to 1990. Only Cup wins by Montreal in 1986 and Calgary in 1989 interrupted the 11-year Islanders-Oilers' reign of the 1980s.

1.23 **D. Anyone in the team organization**

There's no limit on the number of Stanley Cup miniature trophies that can be made and distributed among members of the winning organization. However, each miniature trophy costs $400 and the NHL pays for only 21 trophies. Any additional trophies are paid for by the team itself.

1.24 **B. Al Arbour**

As of 1996, Bowman has 263 games coached and 162 wins in 51 playoff series; or the equivalent of about four regular seasons' worth of post-season work! Arbour is the only other bench boss to reach the 200–100 coaching milestone with 209 playoff games and 123 victories.

Coaching Playoff Games and Wins

Coach	Years	Series	G	W	L	Cups	Pct.
Scotty Bowman	22	51	263	162	101	6	.615
Al Arbour	16	42	209	123	86	4	.589
Dick Irvin	24	45	190	100	88	4	.532
Mike Keenan	11	28	160	91	69	1	.568
Glen Sather	10	27	126	89	37	4	.706
Toe Blake	13	23	119	82	37	8	.689

G O A L I E   G R E A T S

Listed below are the first names of some of hockey's greatest Cup-winning goalies. Once you've figured out their last names, find them in the puzzle by reading across, down or diagonally. Following our example of Gerry M-C-N-E-I-L, connect the other 16 names using letters no more than once. Start with the letters printed in heavy type.

(Solutions are on page 134)

Tom _____   Johnny _____   Turk _____

Frank _____   Gerry _____   Alex _____

Ken _____   Grant _____   George _____

Gump _____   Charlie _____   Rogie _____

Terry _____   Jacques _____   Georges _____

Patrick _____

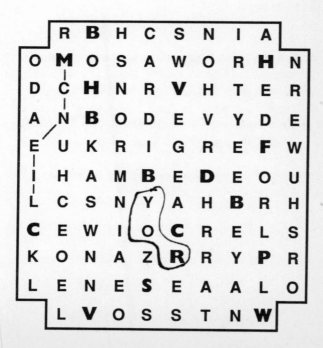

Chapter TWO

LONG BEFORE OUR TIME

This chapter blows the dust from some very old hockey tomes and a library's worth of musty newspaper clippings to search out the really obscure stuff on the origins of the Stanley Cup and its playoff history. From Arthur and Algy to the Dawson City Nuggets, here is everything you always wanted to know about the Cup but didn't know who to ask or where to find out.

(Answers are on page 25)

2.1   **Whose idea was it to create a championship hockey award?**
A. Lord Stanley himself
✔B. Lord Stanley's sons, Arthur and Algy
C. Lord Stanley's wife, Lady Stanley
D. Lord Kilcoursie, Lord Stanley's personal aide

2.2   **In the beginning, who decided if a team was a worthy challenger for the Stanley Cup?**
✔A. The Stanley Cup trustees
B. Executives of the Ontario Hockey Association
C. The previous year's Cup champions
D. Any team that iced enough good players could mount a challenge

2.3 **When Lord Stanley first presented the Cup in 1892, he appointed two trustees to decide who would play for it. How many trustees are there today?**
A. None; the Cup trustee tradition stopped long ago
✓ B. Two trustees
C. 12 trustees
D. 26 trustees, one for each NHL franchise

2.4 **What were used as rink boards in the first Stanley Cup matches?**
A. Fence posts and chicken wire
B. Sandbags piled on top of one another
✓ C. Spectators
D. Cardboard boxes filled with bricks

2.5 **In 1909, the Edmonton Eskimos were accused of putting together a team of "ringers" to win the Stanley Cup. What was a "ringer" at that time?**
✓ A. A paid pro player
B. An aggressive skater known for injuring players
C. A player who could play both forward and defense
D. A player with great endurance

2.6 **In 1914, which western team forgot to file the necessary papers to challenge for the Stanley Cup?**
A. The Vancouver Millionaires
✓ B. The Victoria Aristocrats
C. The Portland Rosebuds
D. The Calgary Cougars

2.7 **What was the name of the team from the smallest community to challenge for the Stanley Cup and win it?**
A. The Renfrew Millionaires
B. The Brandon Wheat Kings
C. The Brockville Badgers
✓ D. The Rat Portage (Kenora) Thistles

1905's plucky Cup challengers from Canada's north.

2.8 **Pictured above is the 1905 team that holds the record for the longest distance travelled to play in the Stanley Cup. What is the team's name?**
A. The Seattle Metropolitans
B. The Vancouver Millionaires
✔ C. The Dawson City Nuggets
D. The Yellowknife Bears

2.9 **Why was the 1899 Stanley Cup series never finished?**
✔ A. The referee and one team left the ice in protest
B. No substitute could be found for an injured goalie
C. No substitute could be found for an injured referee
D. The crowd kept throwing debris on the ice

2.10 **Which trophy became the award for the best amateur hockey team, after professional teams took over the Stanley Cup?**
A. The Hart Trophy
B. The Allan Cup
C. The AHA (Amateur Hockey Association) Award
D. The Silver Stick Award

2.11 **What was so special about the 1916 Stanley Cup finals?**
A. An American team played a French-Canadian team
B. The Stanley Cup finals were played on American soil
C. A western team won the Stanley Cup
D. The series was played without the Stanley Cup trustees' approval

2.12 **Which early (pre-NHL) player holds the records for most playoff goals, most goals in a playoff series and most goals in one playoff game?**
A. Art Ross
B. Billy Barlow
C. Frank McGee
D. Newsy Lalonde

2.13 **How were the Stanley Cup playoff rules changed in 1914?**
A. Amateur teams were barred from Cup competition
B. The finals became a best-of-five series between the NHA and PCHA champions
C. The finals became a three-game total-goals series
D. The regular season was split into halves; winners of each half played for the championship

2.14 **In 1921, which third major hockey league took its place beside the NHL and PCHA, anxious for a crack at the Stanley Cup?**
A. The American Hockey Association
B. The Eastern Hockey League
C. The Western Canada Hockey League
D. The North American Hockey Association

23

2.15 **Why did the NHL take over exclusive rights to the Stanley Cup in 1926?**

    A. Because hockey fans wanted one Cup for one league

  ✔ B. Because the WHL folded, leaving the NHL in charge by default

    C. Because the NHL forwarded an ultimatum to the trustees: Give us the Cup or we'll never play for it again

    D. Because the NHL was the only league with enough money to mount Cup competitions

2.16 **Until 1922, the eastern and western leagues played under different rules. Which rule was alternated when they met in playoff action?**

    A. Whether to use two referees or one referee and one linesman

    B. Whether to play two 30-minute periods or three 20-minute periods

    C. Whether to divide the ice into two or three sections

  ✔ D. Whether to play six-man or seven-man hockey

2.17 **When was the last time a non-NHL team made a formal challenge to the league to play for the Stanley Cup?**

    A. 1932

    B. 1952

    C. 1972

  ✔ D. 1992

LONG BEFORE OUR TIME

2.1 **B. Lord Stanley's sons, Arthur and Algy**

Hockey history is somewhat vague on who inspired Lord Stanley to purchase a trophy, but most references give credit to his sons, Arthur and Algy. Each of Stanley's seven sons were avid sportsmen, but Arthur and Algy became enthralled with hockey when they arrived in Ottawa in 1888. They built a private ice rink on the grounds of Rideau Hall and formed the Rideau Rebels, an amateur team composed of senators, Parliament members, aides de camp and all the Stanley brothers. After they formed the Ontario Hockey Association in 1890, it is believed that they persuaded their father to buy a trophy that would go to the best hockey team in Canada.

2.2 **A. The Stanley Cup trustees**

Lord Stanley appointed two Cup trustees, entrusting them with the following mission: "...to suggest conditions to govern the competition. In case of any doubt as to the title of any club to claim the position of champions, the Cup shall be held or awarded by the trustees as they might think right, their decision being absolute." In the early days, when the Stanley Cup was still a challenge trophy (any team could challenge for the Cup) and not the property of one league, the trustees were almighty, determining Cup challengers, appropriate ice conditions, dates of the championship series and such issues as the number of ringers allowed and which rules would prevail during playoff games. The tradition of two trustees has remained, though today they have little decision-making power.

Lord Stanley, the Cup's founder.

2.3 B. Two trustees

Today the post of Cup trustee is more that of figurehead, with NHL governors making most of the decisions about rules and regulations governing the Cup. However, trustees take their job seriously and stay a good long time. In fact, there have been only nine Cup trustees since 1893. Phillip Ross wins the longevity award: he was a trustee from 1893 until 1940, a span of 47 years! Brian O'Neill and Justice Willard Estey currently hold the two NHL trustee positions.

2.4 **C. Spectators**

There were no real boards as we know them on the first outdoor ice rinks. One-foot boards did surround the rink, but only to form the ice surface and occasionally stop a puck. Above the boards were platform seats for spectators, who often played an integral part in the game, shouting insults or throwing debris at referees and pushing players back into play. Fans enjoyed coming to see Ottawa Silver Seven Harvey Pulford play. On a good day he could check an opponent clear into the second row of seats.

2.5 **A. A paid pro player**

When the Edmonton Hockey Club noticed that pro players were slowly replacing amateurs in Stanley Cup competition, it issued a formal challenge to Stanley Cup trustees in 1908, then went east to buy the best players it could for the playoffs. Many hockey purists protested, believing that the Cup was intended for amateur and community-owned hockey teams. The *Toronto Telegram* observed: "The only thing on the team that belongs to Edmonton are the sticks and uniforms, and they were imported, too." No matter, Edmonton still picked up "ringers" Lester Patrick, Didier Pitre and Tom Phillips, but lost the two-game, total-goals series to the Wanderers 13–10. By 1910, "ringers" in Stanley Cup competition were gone. The Cup trustees ruled that only regular-season players were eligible for the playoffs.

2.6 **B. The Victoria Aristocrats**

In 1913–14, the governors of the National Hockey Association (NHA) and the PCHA decided that the Stanley Cup should change from a challenge trophy, open to any team, to an award given to the playoff winner between the title holders of each league. Their ultimatum: Do it our way or we'll stop competing for the Cup entirely. The trustees capitulated, and in 1914 Lester Patrick's PCHA title holders, the Victoria Aristocrats, came east to meet the NHA champion Toronto Blueshirts. However, it never occurred to Patrick to issue the required formal challenge to the Cup trustees. Clinging to what few shreds of authority they retained, the trustees told Patrick that, without something in writing, the Aristocrats would not be recognized as Cup holders if they won the series. Teams, fans and the press all ignored these warnings and the series was played, without any paperwork. The confrontation between Cup trustees and Patrick never happened because the Aristocrats lost all three games, giving Toronto its first Stanley Cup in 1914, with 5–2, 6–5 and 2–1 wins.

2.7 D. The Rat Portage (Kenora) Thistles

Unlike most Cup challengers, who hailed from a few large Canadian and American cities, the Thistles' home was Rat Portage, later known as Kenora, a tiny railroad town 140 miles east of Winnipeg. The Thistles had only one player over the age of 21 but enough spark and community enthusiasm behind them to mount three Cup challenges between 1903 and 1907. Their first challenge was against the Ottawa Silver Seven in 1903, when they were walloped 10–4 but gained respect for their athleticism. Said Ottawa's Alf Smith, after Rat Portage's second challenge loss in 1905: "If the Cup has to go, there's no team I'd sooner give it to than the Thistles." Finally, in 1907, the Thistles made another attempt, challenging the Montreal Wanderers using "ringers" such as Art Ross of the Brandon Wheat Kings. This move to "build" a team paid off. The Kenora Thistles won the two-game series and the Stanley Cup with a total-goals score of 12–8.

2.8 C. The Dawson City Nuggets

The Nuggets' marathon cross-continent trek during the winter of 1904–1905 (to meet the Ottawa Silver Seven) remains one of hockey's most colourful and enduring sagas. Leaving a full month before the series, with one man short of a team (they finally picked up cover point Lorne Hanna in Manitoba), this group of gold diggers travelled 4,000 miles by foot, bicycle, dogsled, boat and train to Ottawa, arriving just one day before the sched-

1907 Kenora Thistles: The small-town team that won the Stanley Cup.

uled series was to begin. Exhausted after the 23-day jour-
ney, the Nuggets requested a week's postponement to
practise and get ready. Ottawa refused, and the series
began the next day as planned. Ottawa won the first game
of the best-of-three series 9–2, in a contest filled with
cuts, bruises and banishments. The second match established the all-time, single-game Stanley Cup record for
goals scored as Frank McGee pumped 14 goals into the
Nuggets' net, eight in consecutive fashion. Final score:
Ottawa 23, Nuggets 2. Poor in play, poor in pay, the
Nuggets left Ottawa after their two-game whipping and
toured eastern Canada, playing exhibition games to raise
enough money for their long trip home.

2.9   **A. The referee and one team left the ice in protest**
The 1899 playoff series between the Winnipeg Victorias
and the Montreal Victorias was anything but typical for
referee Bill Findlay. During the second and final match,
with only 12 minutes left in regulation time and Montreal
leading 3–2, Bob McDougall slashed Winnipeg's Tony
Gingras across the knee. Findlay whistled two minutes
for McDougall. Winnipeg, furious over the call and
expecting expulsion for McDougall, left the ice in protest.
Findlay, completely taken aback by Winnipeg's behav-
iour, took off his skates and headed home. More than
an hour later, as spectators waited for some sort of con-
clusion, league officials returned with Findlay. He gave
Winnipeg 15 minutes to ice its team or else. Winnipeg
said they would, but only if Findlay threw out
McDougall, citing an 1897 rule that allowed officials to
banish any player not acting in a gentlemanly fashion.
Findlay refused; Winnipeg held firm. So the game, series
and Cup fell to Montreal as the Stanley Cup trustees
upheld the decision of referee Findlay.

2.10   **B. The Allan Cup**
Converting the Stanley Cup from a trophy for Canada's
top amateur team to a professional team award was not a
smooth process. Proponents of amateur hockey felt that
paid professionals would take the sportsmanship and fun
out of hockey. In 1908, the *Vancouver Province* com-
mented on Edmonton "buying" a team to win the Stanley
Cup: "It is no longer a question of local pride and ambi-
tion but a matter of the club that has the most money.
The conditions certainly are rotten and the historic old
Cup now really represents nothing." Stanley Cup trustees
agreed, but teams still added non-local players, paying
them from gate receipts or with free game tickets. In
1908, Sir Montagu Allan of Montreal donated the Allan
Cup to be awarded to the best "completely amateur"
hockey team. This move and the surge of paid players
into the sport established the Stanley Cup as a professional team trophy by 1910.

2.11 **A. An American team played a French Canadian team.**

The first American/French-Canadian final series in Stanley Cup history took place in 1916, when the U.S.-based Portland Rosebuds met the Montreal Canadiens. Each team's makeup was a hot topic of conversation. The Canadiens were essentially French, with stars such as Georges Vezina, Newsy Lalonde and Jack Laviolette. The Rosebuds had Canadian talent but played out of Oregon in the PCHA. Some fans worried that the trophy would no longer be a Canadian symbol of hockey excellence. Thankfully, the Cup trustees took a broader view: "The Stanley Cup represents more than the championship of Canada. It's really the symbol of the championship of the world." The best-of-five series went the distance in Montreal, and the Canadiens nipped their American foes 2–1 in the deciding game to claim their first championship.

2.12 **C. Frank McGee**

McGee was one of the great early players of the game before the NHL was formed in 1917. He holds three major playoff scoring records from 1893 to 1918, many of them coming when his Ottawa Silver Seven outclassed the Dawson City Nuggets in 1905. McGee set the playoff record for most career goals scored: 63 goals in 22 postseason games between 1903 and 1906; the record for most goals in one playoff series: 15 in two playoff games in 1905; and most goals in one playoff game: 14 in a 23–2 thrashing of Dawson City.

2.13 **B. The finals became a best-of-five series between the NHA and PCHA champions**

By 1914, professional hockey teams were attracting bigger crowds and bigger money with each match. The decision to hold the playoffs only between hockey's two pro leagues, the NHA and the PCHA, was made by the leagues' governors, who put their case to the Cup trustees as a fait accompli: Accept or we'll stop challenging for the Cup. The trustees realized they had no choice: fans were eager to see pro players, east versus west games inspired widespread interest and amateur players seemed satisfied with the Allan Cup. The trustees agreed with the governors and the Stanley Cup maintained its status in professional hockey.

2.14   C. The Western Canada Hockey League
The WCHL was born in 1921 and entered the annual Stanley Cup race with four teams from the Canadian prairies: the Regina Capitals, Edmonton Eskimos, Saskatoon Sheiks and Calgary Tigers. This complicated the playoffs because now three leagues, not two, vied for the Cup. At the end of the first three-league season, the PCHA and WCHL champions met to determine the western representative that would head east to play the NHL champions for the Stanley Cup. The next season, the eastern champs went west and won the Cup by defeating the PCHA and WCHL league winners. This system remained until the PCHA folded in 1925, establishing the two-league format again, between the NHL and WHL (formerly the WCHL).

2.15   B. Because the WHL folded, leaving the NHL in charge by default
After a long and proud history of competing against eastern clubs for the Stanley Cup, the last western league, the WHL, folded in 1926. With eastern teams investing more and more cash in arenas and players, the western clubs just didn't have the resources to compete. WHL owners sold all their talent for a combined $258,000, and players such as Dick Irvin, Eddie Shore, Frank Foyston, George Hainsworth, Red Dutton and the Cook brothers headed east. Three new American teams—the Detroit Cougars, Chicago Blackhawks and New York Rangers—were added, making the NHL a 10-team, two-division league and the exclusive owner, by default, of the Stanley Cup.

2.16 **D. Whether to play six-man or seven-man hockey**

Hockey began as a seven-man game and the shift to six players was hotly debated. The rover or point position was dropped by the NHA in 1911. Press reviews were initially unfavourable: "It is slapdash, ping-pong, every-man-for-himself hockey," said the *Ottawa Citizen*. "Individual rushes and the utter lack of team play is the trademark of the bobtailed six-man game," echoed the *Toronto Globe*. Nonetheless, by season's end, six-man hockey was a fact in the east. When Frank and Lester Patrick moved west to found the PCHA in 1911, they used the original seven-man format. Come playoff time, when east played west for the Cup, rules were alternated: the host team playing its rules for games one, three and five; the visiting team using its rules in games two and four.

2.17 **D. 1992**

The days of the Stanley Cup challenger are long gone, but that didn't stop two Cup-crazy hockey fans from formally filing their own challenge with the NHL to play for the Cup in 1992. Upon hearing that NHL players were going to strike just weeks before the playoffs, students Scott Greer and James Hogaboam of Lethbridge Community College in Alberta recruited local players and residents to form the Lethbridge Kodiaks. They sent their application for a challenge match to the NHL offices but were denied based on the 1926 agreement (between the league and the then-trustees of the trophy) preventing non-NHL teams from competing for the Stanley Cup. Happily, 11 days after the strike began a settlement was reached, allowing the regular season to finish and the playoffs to take place.

NHL FIRSTS: IN WHAT YEAR?

Only three players in NHL history have scored four goals in one finals game. Detroit's Ted Lindsay (April 5, 1955) and Montreal's Maurice Richard (April 6, 1957) each did it, but who was first? In this game, we drop the puck for a face-off on NHL firsts and the years in which they happened. The first NHLer to record four goals in a finals game was Newsy Lalonde, who, on March 22, 1919, scored four times in a 4–2 Canadiens win over the Seattle Metropolitans. Match the NHL firsts and the years in which they occurred.

(Solutions are on page 134)

1921	1940	1949	1971	1989	1929	1941
1950	1974	1992	1934	1945	1959	1975
1993	1937	1948	1969	1982	1995	

1. __*1992*__ The first NHL game ever played in June.

2. __*1937*__ The Rangers' Alex Shibicky is awarded the first penalty shot in finals history.

3. __*1971*__ Bobby Orr becomes the first defenseman in NHL history to score three goals in a playoff game.

4. __*1934*__ The Chicago Blackhawks win their first Stanley Cup.

5. __*1989*__ Ron Hextall becomes the first goalie in NHL history to score a playoff goal.

6. __*1959*__ The first and only time no shutouts were recorded in one playoff season.

7. __*1921*__ The old Ottawa Senators become the first NHL team to win consecutive Stanley Cups.

8. _1945_ For the first time in NHL history two rookie goalies, Detroit's Harry Lumley and Toronto's Frank McCool, oppose each other in the finals.

9. _1975_ The Flyers' Bernie Parent becomes the first back-to-back playoff MVP in NHL history.

10. _1929_ For the first time, two American teams, the Boston Bruins and the New York Rangers, clash in the Cup finals.

11. _1993_ Eric Desjardins becomes the first defenseman in NHL history to record a hat trick in the finals.

12. _1950_ Detroit's Pete Babando scores the first Cup-winning goal in overtime of a seventh and deciding game.

13. _1949_ Toronto becomes the first NHL team to win three consecutive Stanley Cups.

14. _1969_ Serge Savard becomes the first defenseman to win the Conn Smythe as playoff MVP.

15. _1941_ The Boston Bruins become the first team in NHL history to capture the Stanley Cup in straight games in the best-of-seven format.

16. _1974_ The Philadelphia Flyers become the first expansion team to win the Stanley Cup.

17. _1940_ New York's Davey Kerr becomes the first goalie to register three shutouts in one playoff series.

18. _1948_ Gordie Howe makes his Stanley Cup debut.

19. _1995_ Dino Ciccarelli becomes the first NHLer to score three power play goals in a playoff game on separate occasions.

20. _1982_ The Canucks become the first team to represent Vancouver in the Cup finals since 1924.

Chapter **THREE**

IN THE FOOTSTEPS OF LEGENDS

To win the Cup, players have to dig deep. As Wayne Gretzky said after his Edmonton Oilers were defeated by the New York Islanders in the 1983 Stanley Cup finals: "That's why they won and we lost. They took more punishment than we did. They dove into more boards, stuck their faces in front of more pucks, threw their bodies into more pileups. They sacrificed everything they had. That's how you win championships." The Stanley Cup makes heroes of a few individuals each year, those that go beyond playing the game to become legends. Others go on to learn and excel later, while some simply deserve being recognized for their commitment. *(Answers are on page 41)*

3.1 **What is the greatest number of player positions one NHLer has played in a single finals series?**
A. Three positions on the forward line
B. Four positions
C. Five positions
✔ D. All six positions

3.2 **What did Maple Leaf Bill Barilko do, against his coach's orders, to score the Cup winner in 1951?**
A. He abandoned his man
B. He refused to pass the puck up-ice
✔ C. He pinched inside the opposition's blueline
D. He took a dive to gain the man advantage

3.3 **Which coach piloted his teams to a record 16 Stanley Cup finals?**
A. Scotty Bowman
B. Jack Adams
C. Toe Blake
✓D. Dick Irvin

3.4 **Which Red Wing was the first NHLer to hold the Stanley Cup in the air and skate around the rink after winning the championship?**
A. Pete Babando
B. Sid Abel
✓C. Ted Lindsay
D. Gordie Howe

3.5 **Mario Lemieux won the Conn Smythe trophy as playoff MVP in 1991. What kept him out of action for most of the regular season?**
✓A. Back problems and surgery
B. A broken foot
C. Retirement
D. Hodgkin's disease

3.6 **How many players have won consecutive Stanley Cups with two different teams?**
A. One player
B. Three players
C. Five players
✓D. 10 players

3.7 **How did the Red Wings' Doug McKay get his "15 minutes of fame" during the 1950 playoffs?**
✓A. He played only one NHL game, during the Cup finals
B. He scored only one NHL goal, scoring against his own team
C. He scored the first shorthanded goal in post-season play
D. He was suspended one game for throwing a dead octopus at a referee

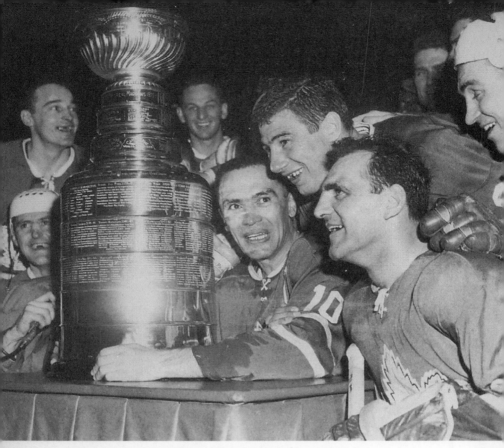

1964 Leafs, after winning their third consecutive Stanley Cup.

3.8 **Pictured above is Toronto's "injured" hero of the 1964 Stanley Cup. Who is he?**
✔ A. Bobby Baun
B. Bob Pulford
C. Frank Mahovlich
D. George Armstrong

3.9 **Why did NHL president Frank Calder hand a life suspension to the Bruins' Billy Couture after the fourth game of the 1927 finals?**
A. He hit a fan with his stick
B. He threatened Calder's life after being fined
✔ C. He assaulted two officials after the game
D. He was caught gambling on the series

3.10 **What is the longest consecutive goal-scoring streak in NHL playoff history?**

A. Six games
B. Nine games
C. 12 games
D. 15 games

3.11 **In 1942, what hockey first did forward Gaye Stewart accomplish?**

A. He jumped from junior to Stanley Cup winner in one year
B. He scored the first Stanley Cup winner by a rookie
C. He posted a shutout as a replacement goalie
D. He netted a natural hat trick to win the final game

3.12 **Who are the four Conn Smythe Trophy winners (playoff MVP) that played for losing teams in the finals?**

A. Roger Crozier, Dave Keon, Bobby Hull and Al MacInnis
B. Jean Béliveau, Glenn Hall, Bill Barber and Chris Chelios
C. Jim Pappin, Rod Gilbert, Reggie Leach and Ray Bourque
D. Roger Crozier, Glenn Hall, Reggie Leach and Ron Hextall

3.13 **Besides Wayne Gretzky, how many other NHLers (as of 1996) have topped the 100-playoff-goal mark?**

A. None
B. One player
C. Two players
D. Four players

3.14 **How many of the original Ottawa Silver Seven made it into the Hockey Hall of Fame?**

A. Three players
B. Four players
C. Six players
D. All seven players

3.15 **In the 1923 playoffs, two Ottawa Senators had brothers playing for the opposite team, the Vancouver Maroons. What families faced off against each other?**

A. The Dennenys and the Bouchers
B. The Patricks and the Broadbents
C. The Gerards and the Cleghorns
D. The Foystons and the Walkers

3.16 **Who was the first recipient of the Conn Smythe Trophy awarded to the MVP of the playoffs?**

A. Glenn Hall
B. Bobby Orr
C. Jean Béliveau
D. Serge Savard

3.17 **What two final-series records does Gordie Howe hold?**

A. Most points/seven-game series and most career penalty minutes
B. Most points/seven-game series and most games played
C. Fastest two goals and most career penalty minutes
D. Fastest two goals and most games played

3.18 **Which Hall-of-Famer had the longest playing career without winning the Stanley Cup?**

A. Bill Gadsby
B. Harry Howell
C. Norm Ullman
D. Marcel Dionne

3.19 **What was unique about Ottawa Silver Seven player Frank McGee, who scored 63 goals in a 22-playoff-game career?**

A. He was only five feet tall
B. He spent his childhood battling tuberculosis
C. He did not start playing hockey until age 14
D. He was legally blind in one eye

IN THE FOOTSTEPS
OF LEGENDS

3.1 **D. All six positions**

Throughout King Clancy's 50 years in hockey, he was never far from the limelight. The tough little Ottawa-born defenseman bluelined for 16 years and with each season his legend grew. In his first Stanley Cup series in 1923, Clancy came aboard to replace injured Ottawa rearguard Eddie Gerard. But the entire Senator squad was suffering: Lionel Hitchman had a broken nose, goalie Clint Benedict was wobbly after being knocked unconscious, and Harry Helman had been hospitalized for a bad cut. Clancy held his own during the two-game final: he played centre and skated on both wings and both sides of defense. His fame was insured when Benedict, penalized for two minutes in game two, handed his stick to Clancy and said: "Here, kid. Take care of this place until I get back." The rookie did as he was told and stopped two shots. Ottawa won the Stanley Cup (defeating the Edmonton Eskimos), and overnight Clancy went from substitute to playoff star.

3.2 **C. He pinched inside the opposition's blueline**

Few teams reach the Stanley Cup finals without a system, and fewer players make it there without following that system. When Toronto met Montreal in the 1951 Cup finals, Leaf coach Joe Primeau played one defenseman back or outside the opponent's blueline to counter any quick turnover and rush by the speedy Canadiens. But Primeau could say little to Leaf rearman Bill Barilko, who, contrary to orders, crossed Montreal's blueline on a gutsy play to score the Cup-winning goal in overtime. Barilko, hanging back as planned, saw the puck squirt away from the net. He gambled and dashed in, putting all his weight into a shot that ripped past Habs goalie Gerry McNeil at 2:53 of overtime. Before the days of the rushing defenseman or pinching on the play, Barilko's manoeuvre was considered daring. Luckily, it worked, proving that there are exceptions to the rule in any system.

3.3 D. Dick Irvin

Irvin's coaching career began in Chicago in 1930–31 when he took his Blackhawks to his first Cup final. Chicago lost, but Irvin rallied the next year, coaching Toronto to a championship. In all, Irvin coached 24 years in the NHL, reaching the finals a remarkable 16 times! Unfortunately, once there, he rarely won: only four Cups in 16 attempts.

Dick Irvin's Trail to the Cup

Year	Irvin's Team	Opponent	W	L	Final
1931	Chicago	Montreal	2	3	Lost
1932	**Toronto**	**New York**	**3**	**0**	**Won**
1933	Toronto	New York	1	3	Lost
1935	Toronto	Maroons	0	3	Lost
1936	Toronto	Detroit	1	3	Lost
1938	Toronto	Chicago	1	3	Lost
1939	Toronto	Boston	1	4	Lost
1940	Toronto	New York	2	4	Lost
1944	**Montreal**	**Chicago**	**4**	**0**	**Won**
1946	**Montreal**	**Boston**	**4**	**1**	**Won**
1947	Montreal	Toronto	2	4	Lost
1951	Montreal	Toronto	1	4	Lost
1952	Montreal	Detroit	0	4	Lost
1953	**Montreal**	**Boston**	**4**	**1**	**Won**
1954	Montreal	Detroit	3	4	Lost
1955	Montreal	Detroit	3	4	Lost

Irvin coached 77 final series games for a 32–45 record.

3.4   **C. Ted Lindsay**
It might have been the climactic seventh-game overtime goal or it might have been the noise thundering down from the Detroit Olympia's rafters, but whatever inspired Lindsay, hockey can thank him for one of its most enduring images. It happened during the Cup presentations of 1950. In a spontaneous act of sportsmanship, Lindsay grabbed the Cup from captain Sid Abel and hoisted it high above his head for a skate around the rink. Budd Lynch of Detroit television recalls: "In the excitement, he just picked up the Cup to get the crowd going. He moved right along the boards so the fans could see the Cup up close. I guess other people saw it because of TV, and it caught on." The "hoisting of the Cup" remains a venerated Stanley Cup tradition.

3.5   **A. Back problems and surgery**
Lemieux's incredible comeback in 1990–91 is a story Stanley Cup legends are made of. After back surgery sidelined him for all but the last 26 regular-season games, Lemieux stormed back in the playoffs. Despite missing one game, he led all scorers in the five-game Pittsburgh–Minnesota finals with 12 points (5–7–12). Lemieux's remarkable performance brought the Penguins their first Cup and earned him the playoff MVP. The next season the relatively healthy Magnificent One repeated the success story with Pittsburgh, winning another Cup and his second MVP honour.

3.6   **D. 10 players**
Many players have earned consecutive championships in their careers, but few have ever captured back-to-back Cups with two different teams. The most recent is Claude Lemieux, who became the first NHLer in 34 years to win successive Cups, with New Jersey in 1995 and with Colorado in 1996. Eddie Gerard accomplished it twice, winning the Cup with the 1921 Ottawa Senators and the 1922 Toronto St. Pats, and then again with the Senators in 1923. Harry Holmes is the only goalie among the group.

Back-to-Back Cup Winners

Player	First Championship	Second Championship
Claude Lemieux	1995 New Jersey	1996 Colorado
Al Arbour	1961 Chicago	1962 Toronto
Ed Litzenberger	1961 Chicago	1962 Toronto
Ab McDonald	1960 Montreal	1961 Chicago
Lionel Conacher	1934 Chicago	1935 Montreal
Eddie Gerard	1922 Toronto	1923 Ottawa
Eddie Gerard	1921 Ottawa	1922 Toronto
Harry Holmes	1917 Seattle	1918 Toronto
Bruce Stuart	1908 Montreal	1909 Ottawa
Art Ross	1907 Kenora	1908 Montreal
Jack Marshall	1901 Winnipeg	1902 Montreal

3.7 **A. He played only one NHL game, during the Cup finals**
Based on a ratio of NHL games played versus Cup victories, McKay has a great average. Called up for the 1950 Red Wings–Rangers finals, McKay lasted one game, just long enough to earn a place on the champion Red Wings. McKay produced no goals, assists or penalty minutes but still holds the distinction of being the sole NHLer to play his only league game with a Stanley Cup winner in the finals.

3.8 **A. Bobby Baun**
Late in game six of the 1964 Detroit–Toronto finals, with the score tied 3–3 and Detroit one goal away from claiming the Stanley Cup, Leafs defenseman Baun is carried off in severe pain after a Gordie Howe slap shot pulverizes his ankle. In overtime, Baun is back on the ice. Within moments, he rifles a shot past Terry Sawchuk for the game winner, a goal that saves Toronto and sends the series to a seventh and deciding game. Two days later, on crutches and ignoring doctors' orders to have his swollen ankle x-rayed, Baun suits up for the final contest. The Leafs cruise to a 4–0 Cup win and he never misses a shift. The

following day, doctors verify by x-ray what Baun himself already presumed. He had scored a playoff game winner and played the entire seventh game on a broken ankle. (In our photo, Baun is in the forefront, holding a stick.)

3.9 **C. He assaulted two officials after the game**
The 1927 Stanley Cup finals produced a tight defensive match-up between Boston and Ottawa, but what stole the headlines was the violence in game four. Several fights broke out, but by far the most serious was Billy Couture's attack on officials Gerry Laflamme and Billy Bell as they headed to the dressing room after the game. The melee was witnessed by NHL president Frank Calder, who had just left his rinkside box to exit the building. While most of the combatants received $100 fines and minor suspensions, Couture was fined $100 and expelled from the NHL permanently. His reinstatement into the league five years later proved too late for a successful comeback.

3.10 **B. Nine games**
Flyer Reggie Leach's record-setting goal-scoring streak began on April 17, 1976, when he potted his first of 14 goals in nine straight games! Leach scored one goal in each of seven games; two in another game; and five on May 6, the last night of the streak, a 6–3 victory over Boston. Leach notched 19 goals during those 16 playoff games in 1976, an NHL record equalled only by Jari Kurri's 1985 playoff output of 19 goals in 18 games.

3.11 **A. He jumped from junior to Stanley Cup winner in one year**
Stewart had a whirlwind season during the 1941–42 schedule. Just 18 years old, he began the year with Toronto's Junior Marlboros, stayed long enough for coffee on the Senior Marlies, then joined the Hershey Bears in the AHL until the Calder Cup playoffs were finished. Then, in April, the Leafs came knocking. Stewart subbed for Henry Goldup in game five, and stayed on in games six and seven to become part of Toronto's come-from-behind

Stanley Cup champions of 1942. As he observed: "What a thrill for a kid still going to high school in Toronto."

3.12 D. Roger Crozier, Glenn Hall, Reggie Leach and Ron Hextall

Since 1965, only four players from losing teams have won the Conn Smythe Trophy as the playoff MVP. Three of the four are goalies: Crozier of the 1966 Red Wings, who posted a low 2.17 goals-against average; St. Louis' Hall in 1968, who went down four straight to the Canadiens' big guns but forced two overtime games; and Hextall, who, in 1987, pushed the Gretzky-led Oilers to seven games. Leach is the only skater so honoured from a losing team. He spearheaded Philadelphia's offensive attack with an all-time record 19 post-season goals, including four in the Cup finals.

3.13 C. Two players

As of 1996, only Wayne Gretzky, Jari Kurri and Mark Messier have reached the 100-playoff-goal plateau in the NHL. Gretzky's milestone marker came against Vancouver on May 7, 1993. Kurri also recorded his 100th during the 1993 playoffs, and Messier did it in 1995.

3.14 C. Six players

The original Silver Seven were goaltender Bouse Hutton, defensemen Harvey Pulford and Art Moore, centre Frank McGee and forwards Harry Westwick, Billy Gilmour and Alf Smith. Moore is the only member of this famous Cup-winning team not in the Hockey Hall of Fame. Although the reign of the Silver Seven lasted barely four seasons, they were an unparalleled collection of athletes, capturing four Stanley Cups between 1903 and 1906. When the original team broke up in 1906, its players went separate ways, some continuing in sports they were already known in: Smith and Hutton in lacrosse; Pulford as a rowing and squash champion; and Westwick, Gilmour and Moore in hockey. McGee retired to the civil service.

1905 Ottawa Silver Seven: Early hockey's toughest, yet most skilled team.

3.15 A. The Dennenys and the Bouchers

Sibling rivalry made for spirited debate in the Denneny and Boucher families come playoff time in 1923. Two sets of brothers—George and Frank Boucher and Cy and Corbett Denneny—faced off against each other in the Vancouver Maroons–Ottawa Senators semifinals that year. George and Cy played for the Senators, while Frank and Corbett skated with the Maroons. While neither of the Dennenys scored playoff goals, both Bouchers notched a pair in the four-game series. (Frank deked out brother George for his two goals.) It was brother against brother, but at least each family had a guarantee that its name went on the Cup!

Detroit's Gordie Howe: The game's best all-round player ever and holder of the NHL record for playoff penalty minutes.

3.16 **C. Jean Béliveau**

The Conn Smythe Trophy was donated in 1964 by Maple Leaf Gardens Ltd. in honour of Conn Smythe, former Leaf coach, manager and owner, as well as the driving force behind the building of Maple Leaf Gardens in 1931. The trophy was first presented during the 1965 Stanley Cup finals to Béliveau, who scored eight goals and collected 16 points in 13 playoff games. In Montreal's march to the Cup, the Habs' captain had three game winners. His most memorable goal came during the final's climactic seventh game, when he set the pace by scoring after only 14 seconds. The momentum catapulted Montreal past Chicago, who never got on the scoreboard during Montreal's 4–0 Cup-clinching victory. Only the Hawks' Bobby Hull scored more often than Béliveau that playoff year, collecting 10 goals for 17 points.

3.17 **A. Most points/seven-game series and most career penalty minutes**

Despite all the playoff records broken by Wayne Gretzky after Howe retired, there are a few Howe still holds, including an offensive mark. Howe scored a record 12 points in seven games during the 1955 Cup finals against Montreal. Three other NHLers, including Gretzky, are tied with 11 points. Howe, a.k.a. Mr. Elbows, also owns the record for most career box time in the finals: 94 minutes in 55 games.

PIM	Player	Team	Games
\multicolumn{4}{l}{**Most Penalty Minutes in Finals**}
94	Gordie Howe	Detroit	55
87	Kevin McClelland	Edmonton	22
86	Duane Sutter	NY Isles	24
83	Maurice Richard	Montreal	59
79	Wayne Cashman	Boston	26
78	Jean Béliveau	Montreal	64

3.18 **B. Harry Howell**

A handful of Hall-of-Famers have never won hockey's most prized trophy during their playing careers, including Howell, who played in only 38 playoff games during his 21-year NHL career. Howell never once moved beyond the semifinals. However, Howell's long, Cup-less playing career was later rewarded. His name is engraved on the Cup as a scout with the Edmonton Oilers.

Cup-Less Hall-of-Famers

Player	Team	Regular-Season GP	Years	Playoffs GP
Harry Howell	NYR/Oakland/LA	1,411	21	38
Norm Ullman	Detroit/Toronto	1,410	20	106
Marcel Dionne	Detroit/LA/NYR	1,348	18	49
Jean Ratelle	NYR/Boston	1,281	21	123
Bill Gadsby	Chi/NYR/Det	1,248	20	67
Gil Perreault	Buffalo	1,191	17	90
Leo Boivin	Tor/Bos/Det/Pit/Min	1,150	19	54

3.19 **D. He was legally blind in one eye**

Many old-timers remember Frank McGee as the greatest player ever. Remarkably enough, all of his scoring feats, such as most playoff goals (14) in a game (against the Dawson City Nuggets in 1905), were set after McGee had already been blinded in one eye. The mishap occurred during a 1900 hockey match played under poor lighting conditions at a Hawkesbury, Ontario, arena. Few details exist, but McGee received a severe eye injury, perhaps from a bad cut by a puck or stick. Just 20 years old, he was forced to retire. Two seasons later, McGee was coaxed back into action and soon established himself as the game's premier player with the Cup-winning Ottawa Silver Seven. Hockey legend Frank Patrick recalls: "He had everything, speed, stickhandling, scoring ability and he was a punishing checker."

STANLEY CUP-WINNING GOALS

Since 1927, 15 different teams have won the Stanley Cup. Match the players in the left column with the teams with which they scored their Stanley Cup-winning goals (in the right column). In this game, all 15 championship clubs are represented, including a few multiple Cup winners such as the New York Islanders.

(Solutions are on page 136)

1. __Q__ Mike Bossy
2. __D__ Uwe Krupp
3. __H__ Howie Morenz
4. __T__ Gordie Howe
5. __N__ Wayne Gretzky
6. __B__ Bobby Orr
7. __P__ Andy Bathgate
8. __L__ Mark Messier
9. __M__ Rick MacLeish
10. __J__ Baldy Northcott
11. __G__ Doug Gilmour
12. __I__ Ron Francis
13. __S__ Cy Denneny
14. __C__ Ab McDonald
15. __O__ Neal Broten
16. __R__ Ted Kennedy
17. __F__ Guy Lafleur
18. __A__ Craig Simpson
19. __E__ Bryan Hextall
20. __K__ Bob Nystrom

A. The 1990 Edmonton Oilers
B. The 1970 Boston Bruins
C. The 1961 Chicago Blackhawks
D. The 1996 Colorado Avalanche
E. The 1940 New York Rangers
F. The 1976 Montreal Canadiens
G. The 1989 Calgary Flames
H. The 1930 Montreal Canadiens
I. The 1992 Pittsburgh Penguins
J. The 1935 Montreal Maroons
K. The 1980 New York Islanders
L. The 1994 New York Rangers
M. The 1974 Philadelphia Flyers
N. The 1988 Edmonton Oilers
O. The 1995 New Jersey Devils
P. The 1964 Toronto Maple Leafs
Q. The 1983 New York Islanders
R. The 1947 Toronto Maple Leafs
S. The 1927 Ottawa Senators
T. The 1955 Detroit Red Wings

Chapter **FOUR**

SCRATCHING THE SURFACE

For the record, there is only one Stanley Cup. But there is a Cup replica that goes on display at the Hockey Hall of Fame in Toronto when the official Stanley Cup is on the road. Although Henri Richard and Toe Blake have each won a record 11 Stanley Cups, another individual has had his name inscribed more often on the Cup. But he's a Montreal Canadien, so you'll have to wait until Chapter 7 to learn his name. In this chapter, we scratch the surface of the Cup's grand history to reveal the little-known details etched into its silverware.

(Answers are on page 56)

4.1   What was the original name of the Stanley Cup?
A. Canadian Hockey Cup
B. Dominion Hockey Challenge Cup
C. Canadian Amateur Hockey Award
D. It has never had any other name but the Stanley Cup

4.2   From the list below, pick the only player whose name has *never* been misspelled on the Stanley Cup.
A. Bob Gainey
B. Eddie Gerard
C. Guy Lafleur
D. George Armstrong

4.3 What was the overall shape of the Stanley Cup before it was redesigned into its current barrel-shaped form?

✔A. A long cigar

B. A narrow pyramid

C. A wide inverted cone

D. An arched human figure

4.4 How many team names have been misspelled on the Cup?

A. None

B. Two teams

✔C. Four teams

D. Eight teams

4.5 Which retired player made it onto the Stanley Cup with his position engraved as "Ass to Press"?

A. King Clancy

✔B. Maurice Richard

C. Gordie Howe

D. Bobby Clarke

4.6 How many teams have had their names inscribed on the inside of the Stanley Cup bowl?

A. None

B. One team

C. Two teams

✔D. Three teams

4.7 Which U.S. team was the first to have its name engraved on the Stanley Cup?

✔A. The Portland Rosebuds

B. The Chicago Blackhawks

C. The New York Americans

D. The Seattle Metropolitans

4.8 How much was the original Stanley Cup bowl worth?

✔A. Less than $50

B. $250

C. $2,500

D. $25,000

4.9 **How many championship teams used one entire collar or band of the Stanley Cup to inscribe all its players' names?**
A. None; all of those collars have been retired.
B. One team
C. Two teams
✓D. Three teams

4.10 **Which player had both his real name and his nickname engraved on the Cup in the same championship year?**
A. Cecil "Babe" Dye
✓B. Walter "Turk" Broda
C. Maurice "Rocket" Richard
D. Wayne "the Great One" Gretzky

4.11 **Whose name was mistakenly engraved onto the Stanley Cup and then removed by the stamping of a series of Xs over the letters?**
A. The son of Ranger manager Lester Patrick
B. The younger brother of Henri and Maurice Richard
C. The son of Dick Irvin, Sr.
✓D. The father of Edmonton Oiler owner Peter Pocklington

4.12 **Which goalie has had his name spelled four different ways on the Stanley Cup?**
A. Turk Broda
B. Grant Fuhr
C. Billy Smith
✓D. Jacques Plante

4.13 **How many mistakes from the original Stanley Cup were corrected on the duplicate Cup when it was made in 1992?**
A. No mistakes were corrected
B. Less than five mistakes were corrected
✓C. More than five mistakes were corrected
D. More than 10 mistakes were corrected

4.14 **In what year was the original Stanley Cup *bowl* (which sits on top of the Cup) retired?**

   A. 1937
   B. 1947
   C. 1957
   D. 1967

4.15 **Which team has used two different names on the Stanley Cup?**

   A. The Montreal Canadiens
   B. The Detroit Red Wings
   C. The Toronto Maple Leafs
   D. The New York Rangers

4.16 **How many collars or bands have been retired from the Stanley Cup and now reside in the Hockey Hall of Fame?**

   A. Four bands
   B. Six bands
   C. Eight bands
   D. 10 bands

4.17 **Which Bruin player did not qualify as a member of Boston's 1970 championship team, but still had his name engraved on the Stanley Cup?**

   A. Milt Schmidt
   B. Derek Sanderson
   C. Ted Green
   D. Don Awrey

4.18 **What 1990s team used the last available space on the Stanley Cup, thereby requiring a new blank band be added to the bottom of the trophy?**

   A. The 1991 Pittsburgh Penguins
   B. The 1992 Pittsburgh Penguins
   C. The 1993 Montreal Canadiens
   D. The 1994 New York Rangers

SCRATCHING THE SURFACE

4.1 **B. Dominion Hockey Challenge Cup**
Based on Lord Stanley's original intent—for a trophy annually challenged for and awarded to the champion of the Dominion of Canada—his original Cup name was perfect. But soon it became "The Stanley Cup," perhaps because the real name, "Dominion Hockey Challenge Cup," was too long and people just naturally associated it with Lord Stanley. As Canada's governor general, Lord Stanley's stay in the Dominion was relatively brief and, ironically, he returned to England before ever witnessing a championship game or the trophy's presentation.

4.2 **C. Guy Lafleur**
Lafleur is the only Cup winner on the list whose name is spelled correctly. The others are immortalized as Eddie Geard (missing the "r" in Gerard) in 1925–26, George Armstong (missing the "r" in Armstrong) in 1963–64 and Bob Gainy (missing the "e" in Gainey) in 1975–76. Other misspellings include Bill Durnan, who turned into Bill Durman in 1945–46, and Tony Esposito, who inexplicably became "P. Fsopito" in 1968–69.

4.3 **A. A long cigar**
The Stanley Cup trophy has been through four reincarnations. The original bowl trophy presented by Lord Stanley in 1893 was used until the early 1900s. When teams ran out of space for their inscriptions, different sized silver collars or bands were added to the bowl's bottom. In 1939, those bands were standardized, and the trophy grew until it was a long cigar shape. In 1948, the trophy was redesigned into a two-piece structure, with the original bowl and collars sitting atop (but removable

EVOLUTION OF THE STANLEY CUP

from) the wider barrel-base with its five bands. The small bands from the cigar-shaped trophy were retired to the Hall of Fame, and in 1958 the Cup became the one-piece structure we know it as today.

4.4 **C. Four teams**

Certainly players have had their names misspelled, but Cup-winning teams? Yes, and more often than once. In 1916, "Montreal Canadiens" was recorded on the Cup as "Montreal Canadians." Then, the "Toronto Maple Leaes" followed in 1963; the "Bqston Bruins" in 1972; and the "New York Ilanders" in 1981.

4.5 **B. Maurice Richard**

A behind-the-desk image isn't quite how the legendary Rocket is remembered, but in 1965, when Montreal won its 12th Cup, Richard was working as the organization's assistant to the president. The abbreviation stamped "Ass to Press" was laughable, especially in connection with Richard, nobody's yes-man on or off the ice.

4.6 **D. Three teams**

The charm of the Stanley Cup, aside from its legacy, lies in its inconsistencies. Attempts to standardize the engravings only began in the 1930s, and earlier teams often chose independently where to put their names. Three teams marked their inscriptions inside the bowl. On the bowl's bottom can be seen "Wanderers Beat Kenora— 1907." Along the walls of the bowl, inscribed with swirls, is "1915 Vancouver Hockey Club" and each player's name. In small letters along the bowl's top inside rim is the third inscription, "Thistles of Kenora 1907."

4.7 **A. The Portland Rosebuds**

Although the Seattle Metropolitans were the first American team to officially win the Stanley Cup (1917), Portland was the first U.S. club to have its name engraved on the trophy. When the Rosebuds defeated the 1915 Stanley Cup champion Vancouver Millionaires for the

PCHA title in 1916, Vancouver handed the trophy to the Rosebuds to take east for the Cup finals against the NHA title-holder Montreal Canadiens. Portland immediately engraved its own accomplishment on the Cup: "Portland Rosebuds, PCHA Champions, 1915–1916." But winning the PCHA championship didn't give Portland the right to inscribe its name on the Cup. That act of unsportsman-like conduct doomed the Rosebuds, who were edged 2–1 in the final match of the tight five-game series against the Canadiens.

4.8   A. Less than $50

Although it seems a pittance today, Cdn.$48.67—or 10 guineas—was a considerable sum in 1892. Lord Stanley entrusted the task of purchasing an appropriate award to a Captain Colvill, who went to England and came back with a squat, fluted bowl made of nickel and alloys. There were two engravings on the bowl when it first arrived: "Dominion Hockey Challenge Cup" and "Lord Stanley of Preston." The bowl sat on one collar that was mounted on ebony.

4.9   D. Three teams

During the 1920s, teams often used an entire collar to engrave their names and the details of their victory. When the Cup was redesigned, only three of the one-team col-lars were kept on the trophy: the 1923–24 Montreal Canadiens; the 1924–25 Victoria Cougars; and the 1925–26 Montreal Maroons. In the case of the 1923–24 Canadiens, the collar lists players, management, coaches, the entire board of directors and each team they beat, including all the scores of both semifinal and final games.

4.10   B. Walter "Turk" Broda

Broda must have played doubly well in the playoffs to earn two mentions on the 1942 Cup. Engraved both as Walter Broda and "Turk" Broda that year, the mistake is astonishing considering Broda had been the Leafs' regu-lar goalie for six seasons.

4.11 **D. The father of Edmonton Oiler owner Peter Pocklington**
Engraved below "1984 Edmonton Oilers" and "Peter Pocklington, Owner" 16 small Xs are stamped over Basil Pocklington's name. Some say the engraver was mistakenly given the list of recipients of miniature Cup trophies instead of the official names' list for the Cup engraving.

4.12 **D. Jacques Plante**
Plante backstopped Montreal every year during the Canadiens' five-year sweep from 1956 through 1960. Yet four versions of his name appear. In 1956, it was "J. Plante"; in 1957, "Jacques Plante"; in 1958, "Jac Plante"; in 1959, "Jacq Plante"; and in 1960, "Jacques Plante."

4.13 **C. More than five mistakes were corrected**
When the NHL requested that a duplicate of the Stanley Cup be made in 1992, silversmith Doug Boffey created an almost exact replica, complete with many of the mistakes and scratches the original Cup had accumulated over the years. While respecting the trophy's long history (warts and all), Boffey did correct the misspellings of George Armstrong, Bob Gainey and Bill Durnan (see Question 4.2), the misspelling of the New York Islanders (Question 4.4), changed "P. Fsopito" to "Tony Esposito" on the 1968–69 inscription (Question 4.2) and dropped the string of Xs under the 1983–84 Oilers engraving (Question 4.11).

4.14 **D. 1967**
Although the overall look and design of the Stanley Cup trophy has changed over the years, Lord Stanley's original bowl from 1892 remained on top of the various Cup bases until 1967. After 75 years of wear and tear, the bowl was quite brittle and susceptible to damage, so NHL president Clarence Campbell asked silversmith Carl Petersen to create an exact duplicate of the original bowl. Only a handful of people knew of the replica, including, of course, its maker, Mr. Petersen. It wasn't until the Stanley

Carl Petersen: The Montreal silversmith who made a new Stanley Cup.

Cup was stolen three years later in 1970 (it was later recovered) that the hockey world was told of the original bowl (which was in safekeeping in the hands of Mr. Petersen). The replica bowl now sits atop the Stanley Cup. The original Cup bowl can be found in the Hockey Hall of Fame.

4.15   ## A. The Montreal Canadiens

Since their first championship in 1916, the Canadiens have used either the English "Montreal Canadiens" or the official French name "Club de Hockey Canadien

Inc." on the Stanley Cup. Logic hasn't played much of a part in determining why one name has been used over another, but at last count the Montreal Canadiens had won the trophy 15 times and the Club de Hockey Canadien Inc. was victorious on nine occasions.

4.16   D. 10 bands

The four design changes to the Stanley Cup over the years have eliminated 10 Cup bands and collars. Some of the bands list only one championship each, while others span a specific era and include many winning teams. For example, missing from the Cup is the 1928–1940 band with the first three Ranger championships.

4.17   C. Ted Green

Few players in the Bruins' history have played with more grit while wearing the famous black-and-gold Boston B than Ted Green. Even though he didn't qualify as part of the 1969–70 champion Bruins (after being sidelined the entire season and playoffs with a fractured skull), the club showed great class by including his name on the players' list that was sent to the Cup engravers. NHL president Clarence Campbell didn't favour the idea, but the Bruins stuck by their eight-year veteran and Green's name was etched into the silverware along with his teammates'.

4.18   A. The 1991 Pittsburgh Penguins

When the Cup was redesigned to accommodate the wider five-band barrel shape in the 1940s, the intention was to have each new band hold 13 teams, running from 1928 to 1992. This format meant that a new band would be required in 1993, the centennial year of the Stanley Cup. However, the 1965 Montreal Canadiens took twice the usual space of 12 square inches. As a result, the five bands were filled by 1991 after Pittsburgh's Cup. In 1992, the first band (1928–1940) was retired to the Hockey Hall of Fame and another band was added, which, if everyone plays along, will last until 2005.

D E F U N C T   T E A M S

Since the Stanley Cup was first awarded to the Montreal AAA in 1893, dozens of defunct teams (from the NHL and elsewhere) have competed for the trophy. Some became Cup champions, such as the Vancouver Millionaires in 1915; many more, such as the 1911 Port Arthur Bearcats, fell into obscurity after failing in their challenges. In this game, we check how closely you've been paying attention in previous chapters. Match the cities below and their Cup-contending teams.   *(Solutions are on page 137)*

1. Vancouver _____	A.	Americans
2. Kenora _____	B.	Thistles
3. Quebec _____	C.	Wheat Kings
4. Pittsburgh _____	D.	Maroons
5. Sydney _____	E.	Rosebuds
6. Ottawa _____	F.	Blueshirts
7. Seattle _____	G.	Nuggets
8. Victoria _____	H.	Victorias
9. Brandon _____	I.	Silver Seven
10. Toronto _____	J.	Pirates
11. Portland _____	K.	Metropolitans
12. Edmonton _____	L.	Millionaires
13. Winnipeg _____	M.	Tigers
14. New York _____	N.	Cougars
15. Calgary _____	O.	Miners
16. Dawson City _____	P.	Eskimos
17. Montreal _____	Q.	Bulldogs

TEAM SPIRIT

In 1967, the Toronto Maple Leafs iced the oldest lineup ever to win a Stanley Cup. The finals pitted Toronto's greybeards against the high-flying defending-Cup champion Montreal Canadiens. Few people gave the Leafs a chance. Toronto's roster sported goalie Johnny Bower, age 42, defenseman Allan Stanley, 41, five other Leafs over 35 and 12 regulars over 30! But, in the playoffs, it's often not the team with the best players that wins, it's the best-playing team that becomes champion. Despite being outgunned and over-the-hill, the '67 Leafs were the top team on the ice. *(Answers are on page 68)*

5.1   **Besides the 1942 Toronto Maple Leafs, name the only other NHL club to win a best-of-seven series after losing the first three games.**
   ✓ A. The New York Islanders
   B. The St. Louis Blues
   C. The San Jose Sharks
   D. The Vancouver Canucks

5.2   **Gordie Howe was describing which championship team of the early sixties when he said: "There's not a bad apple in the barrel."?**
   A. The Detroit Red Wings
   B. The New York Rangers
   ✓ C. The Toronto Maple Leafs
   D. The Chicago Blackhawks

5.3 **Which was the first *NHL* team to win the Stanley Cup?**
    A. The Montreal Wanderers
    B. The Ottawa Senators
    C. The Montreal Canadiens
    D. The Toronto Blueshirts

5.4 **Which team took the shortest time to capture its first Stanley Cup after entering the NHL?**
    A. The Philadelphia Flyers
    B. The New York Islanders
    C. The Pittsburgh Penguins
    D. The Edmonton Oilers

5.5 **In what year did two American teams first compete in the Stanley Cup finals?**
    A. 1919
    B. 1929
    C. 1939
    D. 1949

5.6 **For what style of hockey was the Ottawa Silver Seven renowned?**
    A. Clean, wide-open hockey
    B. The new six-man lineup without the "rover" position
    C. The toughest, roughest games ever played
    D. A slow, cautious defensive style

5.7 **How many U.S.-based teams have won three consecutive Stanley Cups?**
    A. None
    B. One team
    C. Two teams
    D. Three teams

5.8 **Which was the first western team to win the Cup?**
    A. The Portland Rosebuds
    B. The Vancouver Millionaires
    C. The Winnipeg Victorias
    D. The Seattle Metropolitans

5.9 Name the first NHL team to win three consecutive Stanley Cups.
A. The Montreal Canadiens
B. The Ottawa Silver Seven
C. The Montreal Victorias
D. The Toronto Maple Leafs

5.10 What was the name of the last Maritime team to travel west for a Stanley Cup challenge?
A. The Sydney Miners
B. The Halifax Crescents
C. The New Glasgow Cubs
D. The Moncton Victorias

5.11 Who won the first Stanley Cup series played west of Winnipeg?
A. The Vancouver Millionaires
B. The old Ottawa Senators
C. The Victoria Cougars
D. The Edmonton Eskimos

5.12 Which team has won the most Stanley Cup championships?
A. The Toronto Maple Leafs
B. The old Ottawa Senators
C. The Montreal Canadiens
D. The Detroit Red Wings

5.13 Which defunct NHL franchise instigated the league's first playoff player strike?
A. The St. Louis Eagles
B. The old Ottawa Senators
C. The Hamilton Tigers
D. The New York Americans

5.14 Which team holds NHL records for both *most* goals and *fewest* goals in a four-game Stanley Cup final series?
A. The Boston Bruins
B. The Toronto Maple Leafs

C. The Montreal Canadiens
D. The Edmonton Oilers

5.15 **Which team, playing in the best-of-seven format, was the first to win every post-season game in one year?**
A. The 1941 Boston Bruins
B. The 1946 Montreal Canadiens
C. The 1948 Toronto Maple Leafs
D. The 1952 Detroit Red Wings

5.16 **The following four teams appear on the Stanley Cup, but only one club is considered an official Cup winner. Which one?**
A. The 1910 Montreal Wanderers
B. The 1915 Ottawa Senators
C. The 1916 Portland Rosebuds
D. The 1918 Vancouver Millionaires

5.17 **The year 1925 marks the last time a non-NHL team captured the Stanley Cup. Which team holds that honour?**
A. The Regina Capitals
B. The Calgary Tigers
C. The Victoria Cougars
D. The Edmonton Eskimos

5.18 **What do the 1991 Minnesota North Stars, 1982 Vancouver Canucks, 1968 St. Louis Blues and 1961 Detroit Red Wings have in common?**
A. All advanced to the Cup finals with American captains
B. All advanced to the Cup finals with sub-.500 records in regular-season play
C. All advanced to the Cup finals with NHL rookie coaches
D. All advanced to the Cup finals without losing any previous playoff games

T E A M S P I R I T

5.1 **A. The New York Islanders**
In NHL history, only the Leafs and the Islanders have rallied from 0–3 to win a playoff series. Toronto's dramatic comeback in 1942 stands alone in the annals of Cup finals play; but in 1975, the Isles won four straight from the Penguins after a 0–3 start in the quarterfinals. Amazingly, New York almost duplicated the feat in the next playoff round, again losing the first three games of the semifinals to Philadelphia, only to win the next three. The Islanders' hopes for a second consecutive 0–3 come-from-behind victory were dashed in game seven, a 4–1 loss to the Flyers.

5.2 **C. The Toronto Maple Leafs**
Coming from Mr. Hockey, that was a big compliment. Toronto faced Howe's Red Wings twice (and Chicago once) in three Cup finals from 1962 through 1964. The Leafs took three straight championships with a "barrel of apples" that included some of hockey's greatest names: Johnny Bower, George Armstrong, Red Kelly, Dave Keon, Frank Mahovlich, Bob Baun and Tim Horton.

5.3 **D. The Toronto Blueshirts**
In an effort to rid themselves of the Toronto Blueshirts' troublesome owner, Eddie Livingstone, executives of the National Hockey Association (NHA) dissolved the league in 1917 and promptly appointed themselves directors of a new league, the National Hockey League. They may have shut out Livingstone, but bigger problems followed. The Quebec Bulldogs folded before the season began, and the Montreal Wanderers disbanded after only six games when their arena went up in flames. For the newly

formed NHL, it was not a great beginning. In fact, only three teams survived: Ottawa, Toronto and Montreal. The Blueshirts (a.k.a. the Arenas) defeated Montreal 11–6 in a hard-fought two-game total-goals series. (Jack Adams scored his first pro goal in the series.) Toronto then played host to the Vancouver Millionaires, nipping the westerners 2–1 in the fifth and deciding game of the five-game finals. Toronto had its first Stanley Cup and the NHL its first Cup champion, the Blueshirts.

5.4   **D. The Edmonton Oilers**
When the Oilers won the Stanley Cup in 1984, they were in their fifth NHL season. Although they had a few solid WHAers, including Wayne Gretzky, Edmonton's road to success was built around the Great One and a remarkable string of successful drafts. In 1979, in its first NHL draft, Edmonton chose Kevin Lowe 21st, Mark Messier 48th, and Glenn Anderson 68th; in 1980, Paul Coffey 6th, Jari Kurri 69th and Andy Moog 132nd; in 1981, Grant Fuhr 8th and Steve Smith 111th; and in 1983, Jeff Beukeboom 19th and Esa Tikkanen 80th. Within a few years, the Oilers had a nucleus of players that delivered Edmonton its first Stanley Cup; and soon five Cups in just seven seasons. But in the 1990s, the highly talented core of Oilers was traded off, considered too expensive for any one team to bankroll. (Worth noting: the Colorado Avalanche did win the Cup in its first season, 1995–96, but the Avalanche were transplanted from Quebec City, where the Nordiques had a 16-year NHL franchise.)

Fewest Years for New Team to Win Cup

Years	Team	Joined League	Won Cup	Series Outcome
5	Edmonton	1979	1984	4–1 over NYI
7	Philadelphia	1967	1974	4–2 over Bos
8	NY Islanders	1972	1980	4–2 over Phi
17	Atl/Calgary	1972	1989	4–2 over Mtl
17	Que/Colorado	1979	1996	4–0 over Fla

5.5 **B. 1929**

The first all-American Cup final pitted the Boston Bruins against the New York Rangers in 1929's best-of-three series. After defeating Montreal in the first round, the Bruins, backstopped by rookie sensation Tiny Thompson, moved on to meet the defending Cup champion Rangers, led by Bill and Bun Cook and the legendary Frank Boucher. But New York was no match for Boston. With future Hall-of-Famers Dit Clapper and Eddie Shore, the Bruins swept the Rangers in two games to capture Boston's first Stanley Cup.

5.6 **C. The toughest, roughest games ever played**

The Silver Seven was established in 1903 by Alf Smith, an ornery winger who assembled not only Canada's best team but its toughest. Ottawa's style of hockey was so aggressive, it sparked the first debates on game violence. Players went home "bruised and bloodied," and referees took to wearing hard hats for protection. After a gruelling match against the Toronto Marlboros in 1904, the *Toronto Telegraph* reported: "There is no one on the Marlboros or among their followers who hopes for a victory tonight. Players and officials even considered forfeiting the game rather than being hacked to death again." Despite its roughhouse tactics, the Silver Seven became hockey's most powerful team of the age. Between 1903 and 1906 they owned the Stanley Cup. Today, the Silver Seven are widely considered Canada's first national heroes of the game.

5.7 **B. One team**

The New York Islanders became the first (and only) American team in NHL history to win back-to-back-to-back Stanley Cups en route to claiming four successive championships between 1980 and 1983. The Isles reached their pinnacle as a dynasty through astute drafting in the 1970s, picking up Denis Potvin, Mike Bossy, Clark Gillies, Bryan Trottier and John Tonelli in only a few short years. Other dominant players such as Billy Smith

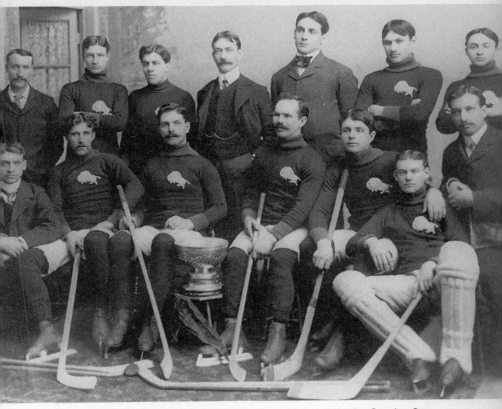

1901 Winnipeg Victorias: The second western team to win the Stanley Cup.

and Butch Goring came through trades. Several U.S. clubs have won consecutive championships, including Detroit, Philadelphia and Pittsburgh.

5.8   **C. The Winnipeg Victorias**
On February 14, 1896, in a one-game, winner-take-all contest between the Winnipeg Victorias and the Montreal Victorias, the westerners beat the defending-Cup easterners 2–0. It was the first Stanley Cup win by a western hockey team and the first shutout game ever in playoff competition. Winnipeg fans gathered at hotels for telegraph reports of the game events in Montreal. When the final score came in, the *Winnipeg Free Press*

reported, "Cheer after cheer went up from the crowd. Everybody wanted to shake hands with everybody else and, for several minutes, old enmities were forgotten in the magnificent victory."

5.9 **D. The Toronto Maple Leafs**

Although the Montreal Victorias and the Ottawa Silver Seven each won the Cup in three consecutive seasons, neither were NHL teams. The honour goes to the 1947–48–49 Maple Leafs. Under coach Hap Day, Toronto was the elite team of the NHL during the 1940s, reaching the finals six times and winning five Cups (including three in a row). The arch-rival Detroit Red Wings were Toronto's favourite victims. The Leafs levelled Detroit 4–1 in the 1947 semifinal series and then won championships in 1948 and 1949, consecutively sweeping the Wings in the minimum four games. As Detroit captain Sid Abel explained: "They pay us to play other teams. We'd play the Leafs for nothing."

5.10 **A. The Sydney Miners**

The Maritime Professional League, with teams in Halifax, New Glasgow, Moncton and Sydney, regularly challenged for the Stanley Cup during the early 1900s. Despite suffering some staggering losses in the total-goal playoff format, the teams from Atlantic Canada remained popular and continued to vie for the Cup until the league folded in 1913. The last east coast challenger was the Sydney Miners, who were humiliated 20–5 by the Quebec Bulldogs in 1913.

The Maritime Professional League

Year	Team	Final Score (two-game total)
1900	Montreal Shamrocks vs. Halifax Crescents	21–2
1906	Montreal Wanderers vs. New Glasgow Cubs	17–5
1912	Quebec Bulldogs vs. Moncton Victorias	17–3
1913	Quebec Bulldogs vs. Sydney Miners	20–5

1915 Vancouver Millionaires: The first west coast Cup winners.

5.11 A. The Vancouver Millionaires

West coast hockey fans saw their first Stanley Cup series in 1915. The game had come west and with it money players like Cyclone Taylor and Frank Nighbor, who played for Frank Patrick's Millionaires in the Patrick-owned Denman Street Arena, the largest rink in Canada at the time. The three-game playoff series between the Ottawa Senators and Vancouver was a rout. The Millionaires trounced Ottawa 6–2, 8–3 and 12–3 to claim the west coast's first Stanley Cup and establish the PCHA as serious Cup challengers. The *Vancouver Sun* reported: "Vancouver clearly and cleanly fulfilled every claim to superiority over the Easterners." Because of the large gate (20,000 fans in three games), Vancouver players earned $300 in Cup money; the Senators $200.

5.12   C. The Montreal Canadiens

This contest isn't even close. The Canadiens have celebrated 24 Stanley Cups, almost twice the number of
championships won by any other NHL team. Most of their
Cups came after Frank Selke was hired as general manager in 1948. He built the NHL's deepest farm system to
produce the league's most enduring dynasty, the five-time
Cup winners from 1956 to 1960. Selke then passed the
reins to manager Sam Pollock, who brought Montreal
two more dynasties during the 1960s and 1970s. The
Canadiens first appear on the Cup as winners of the 1916
NHA–PCHA championship series. The club's most recent
Cup came in 1993, appropriately, on the 100th birthday
of Lord Stanley's trophy.

5.13   C. The Hamilton Tigers

The NHL's first player strike occurred after the 1924–25
regular season, when the first-place Tigers refused to participate in the playoffs without financial compensation.
Their ultimatum? Pay each player $200 more or we won't
show up in post-season. NHL president Frank Calder
refused, ordering the Tigers to play or risk suspensions
and fines for breaking their contracts, which required
their services from December 1 to March 31, a period
that included the playoff schedule. Neither side budged.
The Tigers were disqualified from playoff action and
the players suspended and fined $200 each. The next sea-
son, after the Hamilton franchise folded, the suspended
players were allowed to join other teams only if they had
paid their fines and handed a written apology to Calder.
Hamilton has not held an NHL franchise since.

5.14   A. The Boston Bruins

Interestingly, the Bruins hold (or tie) the records for both
the most and the fewest goals in a four-game final series,
spread 43 years apart. Boston registered the fewest goals
in the 1927 best-of-five series against Ottawa, and also
established the best record, scoring 20 goals against the
Blues in 1970.

Most Goals by One Team in a Four-Game Final

Goals	Team	GA	Opponent	Year
20	Boston Bruins	7	St. Louis	1970
18	Detroit Red Wings	11	Toronto	1936
18	Toronto Maple Leafs	7	Detroit	1948
18	New York Islanders	10	Vancouver	1982
18	Edmonton Oilers	9	Boston	1988

Fewest Goals by One Team in a Four-Game Final

Goals	Team	GA	Opponent	Year
2	Boston Bruins	7	Ottawa	1927
2	Montreal Canadiens	11	Detroit	1952
3	St. Louis Blues	12	Montreal	1969

5.15 D. The 1952 Detroit Red Wings

The first time in NHL history that a team swept both the semifinal and final series in the seven-game playoff format was in 1952, when Detroit posted back-to-back, four-game sweeps, blanking Toronto in the first round and Montreal in the Cup finals. Terry Sawchuk distinguished himself by recording an amazing four shutouts in eight games and limiting the Canadiens to just two goals in the finals. The 1952 playoffs also marked the first time Gordie Howe registered post-season goals in Cup finals action.

5.16 A. The 1910 Montreal Wanderers

Unlike most championship teams (including the 1910 Wanderers) who earned their silverware, three teams in Stanley Cup history awarded themselves the Cup without officially winning it! In 1915, the Ottawa Senators defeated the Wanderers for the NHA title and added their names to the Cup before playing—and losing to—the western champion PCHA Vancouver Millionaires in the official Cup finals. In 1916, the same thing occurred: the Portland Rosebuds beat the Millionaires for the PCHA championship but lost to Montreal in the real final series. In 1918,

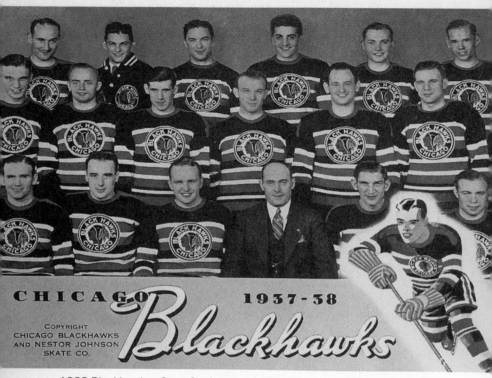

CHICAGO 1937-38 *Blackhawks*

COPYRIGHT
CHICAGO BLACKHAWKS
AND NESTOR JOHNSON
SKATE CO.

1938 Blackhawks: One of only two sub-.500 teams to win the Stanley Cup.

Vancouver upset the reigning Cup-champion Seattle Metropolitans for the league championship. Vancouver had no sooner finished its Cup engravings when the Toronto Blueshirts knocked them off in the finals.

5.17 C. The Victoria Cougars

It was a sweet playoff victory for Lester Patrick's Victoria Cougars in 1925. Patrick's team won the final series against the Montreal Canadiens as much on strategy as on talent, with the east-west game rules deciding the issue. At the time, eastern rules allowed player changes only after the ref's whistle had blown. This suited the Canadiens all-star lineup of 60-minute men such as Howie Morenz, Aurel Joliat and Sprague Cleghorn, who were renowned for their endurance. Patrick, on the other hand, had perfected smooth, quick, on-the-move line changes that, under western rules, were allowed as play continued. When western rules were played in alternate games, the Canadiens were confused. When eastern rules applied, Patrick smartly had his team stop play frequently to make line changes, frustrating the Canadiens who were used to wearing down their opponents. The Cougars won the Stanley Cup in six games, and Patrick's on-the-fly line changes became an integral part of game strategy.

5.18   **B. All advanced to the Cup finals with sub-.500 records in regular-season play**

In NHL history, 15 sub-.500 clubs have reached the Stanley Cup finals. Eleven of the 15 teams finished their regular sked in the last playoff position. Only two sub-.500 clubs, the 1938 Hawks and the 1949 Leafs, won the Stanley Cup.

Sub-.500 Teams in Cup Finals

Year	Team	Season Record	Finish
1991	Minnesota North Stars	27–39–14	16th/21 teams
1982	Vancouver Canucks	30–33–17	11th/21 teams
1968	St. Louis Blues	27–31–16	8th/12 teams
1961	Detroit Red Wings	25–29–16	4th/6 teams
1959	Toronto Maple Leafs	27–32–11	4th/6 teams
1958	Boston Bruins	27–28–15	4th/6 teams
1953	Boston Bruins	28–29–13	3rd/6 teams
1951	Montreal Canadiens	25–30–15	3rd/6 teams
1950	New York Rangers	28–31–11	4th/6 teams
1949	Toronto Maple Leafs*	22–25–13	4th/6 teams
1944	Chicago Blackhawks	22–23–5	4th/6 teams
1942	Detroit Red Wings	19–25–4	5th/7 teams
1939	Toronto Maple Leafs	19–20–9	3rd/7 teams
1938	Chicago Blackhawks*	14–25–9	6th/8 teams
1937	New York Rangers	19–20–9	6th/8 teams

* Won the Stanley Cup.

THE HOCKEY CROSSWORD

Across

1. Canucks 1994 Cup finalist captain
4. 1980s 12-year veteran with Boston, Toronto and Vancouver, Tom _____
7. 1993 Habs Cup winner from Kingston, Ontario
8. 1980s 10-year Ranger Jan _____
9. 1950s Ranger Pat _____
12. Camille Henry's nickname
13. 1980s and '90s nine-year veteran Herb _____
15. _____ spirit
17. Shots _____ goal
18. Jockstrap
19. Winning teams draw big _____
21. Elmer _____
23. 1971 Conn Smythe-winner Ken _____
26. Toronto and Hartford's Rick _____
27. Dishing out the _____ to the body.
28. Used in "The Wave."
29. 1986 Cup-winner _____ Walter
30. 1966 Conn Smythe-winner Roger _____
31. 1987 Conn Smythe-winner _____ Hextall
33. Area in front of net
35. 1940s and '50s two-time Red Wing Cup-winner Joe _____
37. Chico _____
38. _____ for it!
39. Owen _____
41. A New York player is a _____
44. Hometown of the Kings
46. A _____ effort, one-man show
50. Lars from Vancouver and Minnesota
52. Quebec, New York and Tampa's Normand _____
54. _____ Van Impe
55. Hitting the goalpost, a _____ goal

Down

1. Montreal's Yvon _____
2. Players' union
3. Edmonton's _____ Coliseum
4. Two first names of Lord Stanley
5. 1980s and '90s Toronto/Boston wing Dave _____
6. 1970 Boston coach Harry _____
10. Rangers' Sergei _____
11. Lafleur's nickname
14. Full name of Oiler Cup-winning goalie, later with Dallas
16. _____ Tikkanen
20. Winnipeg/Edmonton D-man Fredrik _____
21. 1920s and '30s two-time Cup-winner with Montreal and Chicago, Wildor _____
22. 1970s Montreal/Detroit/Kansas City's Guy _____
24. New _____ Rangers
25. Seven-team coach Harry _____
32. Devils Cup-winner _____ Broten
34. _____ de force
36. 1970s Islander/Blue Ritchie _____
37. 1969 Montreal Cup-winning coach Claude _____
40. _____ -timers
42. 1940s Detroit Cup-winning Captain Sid _____
43. Thug
45. An injury requires first _____
47. The Great _____
48. 1970 and 1972 Conn Smythe-winner Bobby _____
49. _____ pack
51. Boss of team (abbr.)
53. Coast _____ coast

(Solutions are on page 137)

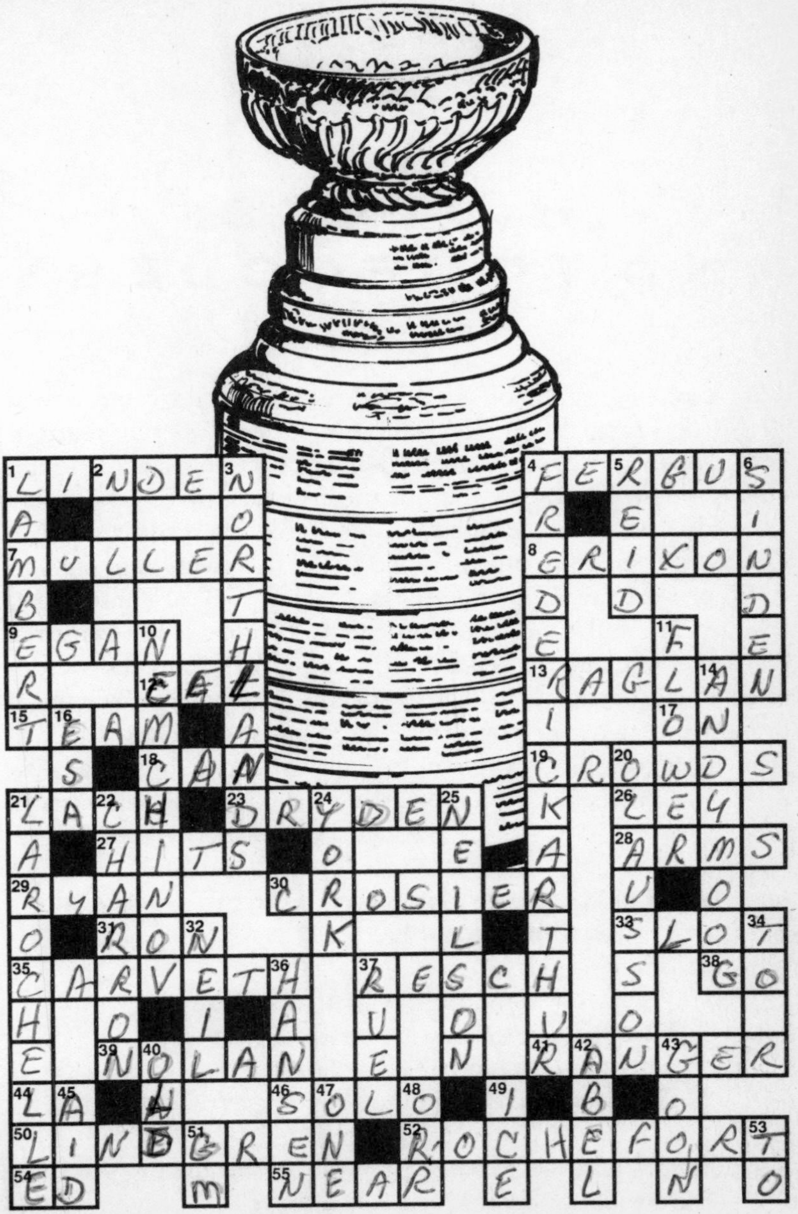

Chapter SIX

HIJINKS AND TOMFOOLERY

Despite being the object of dedicated pursuit for more than 100 years, the Stanley Cup has suffered its fair share of abuse and damage at the hands of its victors. Although champions have sipped champagne from its silver bowl, they have also bashed it around, using it for everything from a flowerpot to a submarine in Mario Lemieux's swimming pool.

To protect the Stanley Cup, the Hockey Hall of Fame began employing a full-time Cup escort in 1994, after it was returned cracked, loose and dented from the New York Rangers' victory tour. The escort plays bodyguard to the trophy while keeping a low profile at the celebrations. Afterwards, the Cup is locked away in its own protective trunk, ready for travel to its next destination. In this chapter, we check out the Cup's checkered past.

(Answers are on page 84)

6.1 **What did Lester Patrick's sons do to the Stanley Cup after their father won it in 1925?**
   A. They tried to sell it
   B. They carved their initials into it with a nail
   C. They used it to keep lemonade in at their refreshment stand
   D. They took it to school to show their friends

6.2 **Where was the Stanley Cup left and forgotten after the Montreal Canadiens won it in 1924?**

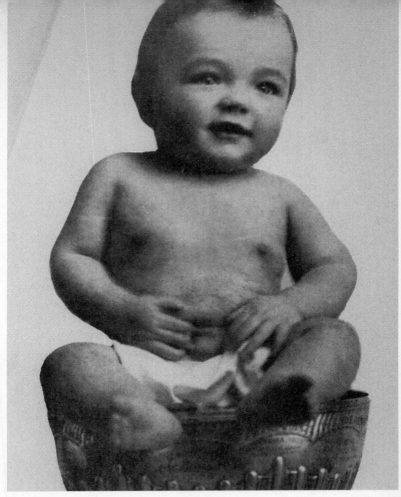

Babysitting the Stanley Cup in 1916: Two causes for celebration.

A. On a Montreal tramway bus
B. On a street curb in Montreal
C. In a player's duffel bag at the Montreal train station
D. In the trainer's room at the Montreal Forum

6.3 **In the photo above, who is sitting in the Stanley Cup?**

A. The daughter of Canadian prime minister Wilfred Laurier
B. The son of King Clancy
C. The only daughter of Lord Stanley
D. The son of Georges Vezina

6.4 **For what purpose did referees King Clancy and Bill Chadwick use the Cup during the 1942 playoffs?**
A. They used it to smuggle illegal liquor across the border
B. They used it to hold poker chips during card games
C. They filled it with hot water, to soak their feet
D. They used it to hold extra pucks and whistles

6.5 **What happened to the Stanley Cup bowl after the Ottawa Silver Seven celebration party in 1905?**
A. It was painted black and gold, the Silver Seven colours
B. It was hidden in the Peace Tower on Parliament Hill
C. It was used as collateral for a taxi ride home
D. It was drop-kicked into the Rideau Canal in Ottawa

6.6 **On which television show did the Stanley Cup appear after the Rangers won the 1994 championship?**
A. *Late Night with David Letterman*
B. *Coach's Corner* with Don Cherry
C. *ABC's Wide World of Sports*
D. *The Tonight Show* with Jay Leno

6.7 **To what unique purpose was the Cup put in 1906?**
A. A radio antenna
B. A serving bowl for punch
C. A flowerpot
D. A spittoon

6.8 **Where was the stolen Stanley Cup collar found, after it went missing for seven years during the 1970s?**
A. In a New York City dumpster
B. In a Toronto laundry
C. In a restaurant storage room in Chicago
D. In a Detroit safety deposit box

6.9   What did a Kenora Thistles' executive intend to do with the Stanley Cup before the 1907 final series?

A. Throw it into Lake of the Woods, Ontario

B. Stamp his own name on it

C. Auction it off for a Kenora charity

D. Use it to knock out a Stanley Cup trustee

6.10   Why did a fan steal the Stanley Cup from Chicago Stadium during the 1962 playoffs?

A. He stole it because he was drunk

B. He stole it as part of a fraternity initiation

C. He stole it to impress his girlfriend

D. He stole it because he felt the Cup should stay in Montreal

6.11   What did Guy Lafleur do with the Cup after kidnapping it to his hometown of Thurso, Quebec?

A. He used it to hold condiments at his backyard barbecue

B. He set it on the front lawn for passersby to admire

C. He brought it to a county fair

D. He played a round of golf with it on his cart

6.12   For what odd purpose did New York's management use the Stanley Cup after the 1940 finals?

A. They kept all the players' contracts in it

B. They let Barnum & Bailey's circus use it in its trapeze act

C. They used it as collateral on next season's ticket sales

D. They stuffed legal papers in it and set fire to them

6.13   Mark Messier has his own tradition with the Stanley Cup. Where did he take it after both the 1988 Oilers' Cup victory and the Rangers' win in 1994?

A. To his bed

B. To a private party on a chartered jet

C. To a strip club

D. To an all-night pizza parlour

HIJINKS AND TOMFOOLERY

6.1   **B. They carved their initials into it with a nail**

As kids of the famous hockey pioneer Lester Patrick, Muzz and Lynn dreamed of being hockey champions themselves one day and took an early opportunity to be immortalized on the Stanley Cup. They scratched their names on the Cup after their father won it as manager/coach of the Victoria Cougars in 1925. Like father, like son. Years later, both had their names officially inscribed on the trophy as members of the 1939–40 Cup-winning New York Rangers.

6.2   **B. On a street curb in Montreal**

In 1924, Cup-winning Habs owner Leo Dandurand invited the Canadiens players over to his house for a celebratory drink. With the Cup in tow, Georges Vezina, Sprague Cleghorn and Sylvio Mantha all crammed into Dandurand's Model-T and headed up Côte St. Antoine hill in Montreal. When the car refused to go any farther, everyone got out to push, placing the Stanley Cup on the curb while they worked. The car finally made it up the hill, and the three jumped back in for the drive to Dandurand's house. Only much later, once they realized it was missing, did Dandurand and Cleghorn rush back for the missing trophy. Fortunately, it was still on the same curb.

6.3   **D. The son of Georges Vezina**

In 1916, Vezina had two reasons to be proud. He was the Stanley Cup-winning goalie with the champion Montreal Canadiens and the brand-new father of Marcel Stanley Vezina. (Obviously, Vezina took inspiration from the Cup for his son's middle name.)

The crowning achievement of the Patricks, hockey's "Royal family."

6.4 **B. They used it to hold poker chips during card games**
According to Bill Chadwick, during the 1942 playoffs, league president Frank Calder gave the Cup to Chadwick and Clancy with the words, "Just don't lose it." So the boys in stripes kept it within eyesight, often using it to hold poker chips during their long train rides between NHL cities.

6.5   **D. It was drop-kicked into the Rideau Canal in Ottawa**

In the Cup's 100-year history, no reckless act is more famous than when members of the Silver Seven drop-kicked the trophy onto the ice of the Rideau Canal in 1905. They foolishly left it there overnight. The next morning, club officials inquired as to the trophy's whereabouts. Star forward Harry Smith went back and crawled onto the Canal to retrieve it. As the story goes, Smith then took it for the customary engravings. It was not seen again until the following season's playoff, when someone remembered the Canal antics from the preceding year. Again the finger was pointed at Smith, who searched his house. He found it unceremoniously tucked away in a closet. Not a grand showcase for Lord Stanley's Cup, but far safer than the icy surface of the Rideau.

6.6   **A. *Late Night with David Letterman***

Following the Rangers' Cup victory in 1994, the trophy made a surprise guest appearance on David Letterman. During the show's monologue, Letterman casually leaned back, looked over at his desk and said to band leader Paul Schaefer: "Hey Paul, what's that behind my desk?" Of course, everyone knew something was up. Letterman walked over and pulled out the Stanley Cup to wild applause. He then brought out Mark Messier, Brian Leetch and Mike Richter. After a brief interview with the trio, Letterman placed the Cup onstage, where it remained for the entire show, in front of 20 million viewers.

6.7   **C. A flowerpot**

The Stanley Cup has a bountiful legacy of odd stories. None, however, is as fertile as the one about how it was purposely left (or forgotten, depending on the storyteller) at a photographer's house after the Wanderers won the championship in 1906. After the photo session was finished and the team long gone, someone had the creative idea of using the Cup as a pot for flowers. When the Wanderers searched for the Cup the following spring, it took some time to recall its whereabouts. It was eventually retrieved and emptied of its earthy contents, just in time for the finals against the Kenora Thistles in 1907.

6.8 **B. In a Toronto laundry**
The case of the missing Stanley Cup collar took seven years to solve and some details are still sketchy today. Here are the facts. In 1970, the original three-tiered Cup collar was heisted from the Hockey Hall of Fame. Shortly after the theft, a woman called police to plead for reduced sentences for the thieves in exchange for the Cup collar. When police refused to negotiate, no further word was heard from the mysterious caller. Another seven years passed before a tip-off in 1977 led police to a laundry on Woodbine Avenue in Toronto. The 1925 collar was finally found, wrapped in brown paper and no worse for wear. New markings on the collar eventually broke the case. Apparently, the thieves couldn't resist etching their own names between those of the players.

6.9 **A. Throw it into Lake of the Woods, Ontario**
The 1907 playoffs between the Kenora Thistles and the Montreal Wanderers were filled with controversy. First, Cup trustee William Foran declared the Thistles' arena too small for a championship game and ruled that the series be played in Winnipeg. Then, Montreal lodged a complaint when Kenora added Ottawa stars Alf Smith and Harry Westwick to its roster. Foran backed up Montreal's objection, ruled the two players ineligible and told Kenora the team would be forced to forfeit the Cup if it won. One Thistles executive was so angry he grabbed the cherished trophy and headed to the dock, intending to throw it into Lake of the Woods. Luckily, he was intercepted and the teams, ignoring Cup trustee Foran's threats, worked out their own compromise: Kenora agreed to play the games in Winnipeg and Montreal would permit Smith and Westwick on the ice. Finally, the two-game, total-goal series was played, with the Wanderers outscoring the Thistles 12–8.

6.10   **D. He stole it because he felt the Cup should stay in Montreal**

After the Canadiens were eliminated in Chicago at the 1962 semis, Habs fan Ken Kilander was so distressed he smashed the glass case protecting the Cup in the Stadium lobby, grabbed the trophy and exited out a door, past shocked spectators. But he didn't get far. He was quickly wrestled down by ushers and held until the police arrived. In court the next day, Kilander explained: "Your Honour, I was simply taking the Cup back to Montreal where it belongs."

6.11   **B. He set it on the front lawn for passersby to admire**

Lafleur actually caused some tense moments for club officials after the 1979 finals when he "borrowed" the Cup during an afternoon downtown tour. Unnoticed, Lafleur slipped away with the trophy and drove to his parents' home in Thurso, Quebec. He placed the Cup conspicuously on the front lawn and watched as hundreds of people from miles around paraded past it. After an afternoon of picture-taking, Lafleur returned to Montreal, much to the relief of officials who were still panicked over the Cup's disappearance. Lafleur was reprimanded for his prank, but only for appearances' sake. What could the club do to hockey's greatest scorer of the late 1970s?

6.12   **D. They stuffed legal papers in it and set fire to them**

In January 1941, Madison Square Garden president John Reed Kirkpatrick held a press conference to announce the final payment on the $3-million mortgage on MSG. To celebrate, Kirkpatrick stuffed the mortgage certificate into the Stanley Cup (won the previous spring) and lit a match. Veteran coach Lester Patrick was shocked: "You drink champagne from the Stanley Cup. You kiss it. You embrace it. You pet it. You fawn over it. With arms raised high, you carry it around the rink proudly. But you don't desecrate it by using it as a furnace. No good will come of this." Patrick couldn't have imagined how prophetic his words would prove to be. The Rangers waited more than

The first metamorphosis of the Cup: A new three-tiered silver collar base.

a half-century before winning another Cup, breaking what was known as "The Curse" in 1994.

6.13 C. To a strip club
Messier's post-victory tradition began in 1988 when he took the Stanley Cup to an Edmonton strip club. After 1994's Ranger championship, Messier repeated the custom and took the Cup to Scores, a New York strip joint, where it became a part of the striptease act. Club spokesperson Lonnie Hanover said, "It was the first time I'd seen our customers eager to touch something besides our dancers."

SEVENTH HEAVEN OR HELL

Only 10 Stanley Cup final series have ever gone to the seventh and deciding game. Each decade since the 1940s has featured at least one seven-game playoff final round, with Detroit and Toronto each copping three Stanley Cups in seven games, Montreal two championships, and Edmonton and the New York Rangers one Cup each after winning game seven.

The big losers were Detroit, Montreal and Chicago, who lost two Cups each after seventh-game defeats. Perhaps the most important factor is home-ice advantage. Teams playing at home in game seven have won the Cup eight of 10 times. The most recent team taken to the wall in the seventh game was the New York Rangers, who managed to squeak by the Vancouver Canucks 3–2 in 1994. It was the fourth time the Cup was decided by a one-goal margin.

The hockey words (or combination of words) below appear in the puzzle horizontally, vertically or backwards. Some are easily found, such as FLYERS (who lost their own Cup-deciding seventh game in 1987). Others require a more careful search. After you've circled all 41 words, read the remaining letters in descending order to spell the name of the goalie whose mask appears in our puzzle sketch.

(Solutions are on page 138)

AMATEUR
ARTHUR
BLACKHAWKS
BLUESHIRTS
BOSTON
CANADIENS
CAPTAIN
COACH
COMPETITION
CUP
FINAL
FLYERS
FORWARD
GAME

GLOW
GOVERNOR
HABS
HOCKEY
ISLANDERS
KENORA
LEAGUE
LORD
MAPLE LEAFS
METROPOLITANS
MILLIONAIRES
MONTREAL
NEW YORK
NIGHT

OILERS
OWNER
PLAYER
RANGERS
RINK
SCORE
SEATTLE
SERIES
SILVER SEVEN
ST PATS
SYMBOL
TORONTO
VANCOUVER

```
S
Y  L
M A E T
B N M O A I                H C A O C
O I A R M S N              E U G A E L
L F G O A L I E M        I S T P A T S
S S Y N T A G O V E R N O R E N W O
K E E T E N H P K E L A E I P O E E
W R K O U D T R L V S T N W L U I R
A I C S R E Y L F A A R T G Y E C O
H A O S E R I E S O Y N E A E O R C
K N H B O S T O N C R E C V E R R S
C O M P E T I T I O N W R O L S S K
A I S F A E L E L P A M A U U I H E
L L A E R T N O M T K N I R H V S N
B L U E S H I R T S E L O R D T E O
N I A T P A C A N A D I E N S R R R
S M E T R O P O L I T A N S B A H A
```

THE BIRTHPLACE
OF HOCKEY

Although the Canadian cities of Halifax and Kingston each have long histories with hockey and its parent sports—old games such as hurley and shinny—they are not the sites of the first organized matches using pucks, sticks and rules. Ice hockey originated in Montreal, evolving from old English stick-and-ball games but played with skates on ice. What resulted was a distinctive sport using a flat rubber disk, the first flat-bladed heeled stick and rules adapted from rugby, lacrosse and soccer.

Montreal men moved the game indoors, invented early goal nets and limited the number of players per side. They spread the game to other parts of Canada, including Ottawa, where Lord Stanley was persuaded to donate a trophy to the champions of the Dominion.

As the economic centre of Canada, Montreal became the unofficial capital of hockey, only to be later surpassed by Toronto and New York. On the ice, early Montreal teams, sometimes three or four to a league, dominated the Stanley Cup playoffs. The Canadiens followed that tradition by setting the professional record for team championships with 24 Stanley Cups.

In this chapter, we focus on the enduring legacy of Montreal clubs and their dominance in Stanley Cup play.

(Answers are on page 97)

7.1 **How many different Montreal teams have won the Stanley Cup?**
A. Three teams
B. Four teams
C. Five teams
D. Six teams

7.2 **Which was the first club to challenge the Montreal AAA for the Stanley Cup?**
A. The Ottawa Capitals
B. Toronto's Osgoode Hall Law School
C. The Ottawa Silver Seven
D. Montreal's McGill University

7.3 **Which individual's name appears most often on the Stanley Cup?**
A. Maurice Richard
B. Trainer Ed Palchak
C. Henri Richard
D. Jean Béliveau

7.4 **What memento did each player on the 1893 champion Montreal AAA receive along with the Stanley Cup?**
A. A gold and silver pocket watch and chain
B. A miniature replica of the Cup
C. A silver-plated hockey stick
D. A gold ring

7.5 **To claim four Stanley Cups from 1976 to 1979, the Canadiens had to play between 16 final series games (four games per final to win four Cups) and 28 games in the four best-of-seven final series of 1976, 1977, 1978 and 1979. How many games *did* Montreal play in total during those four final rounds to win four Cups?**
A. 16 final series games
B. 19 final series games
C. 22 final series games
D. 25 final series games

7.6 **What famous Canadiens line was responsible for 10 of the 16 goals in the 1944 finals?**
A. The Rocket Line
B. The Punch Line
C. The Flying Frenchmen
D. The Goal Line

7.7 **How did Montreal manager Leo Dandurand discipline his roughest players during the 1923 playoffs?**
A. He traded away his most penalized players
B. He imposed fines and suspended the players himself
C. He made each player apologize to fellow teammates
D. He forced his most penalized players to skate laps

7.8 **Which was the first team to win the Stanley Cup in the Montreal Forum after it opened in 1924?**
A. The Montreal Maroons
B. The Victoria Cougars
C. The New York Rangers
D. The Montreal Canadiens

7.9 **After the 1954 Cup finals, the Montreal Canadiens refused to participate in what long-standing tradition?**
A. As winners, they didn't carry the Cup in the visitor's rink
B. As losers, they refused to shake hands with the winners
C. As losers, they gave no press conference
D. As winners, they celebrated with beer instead of champagne

7.10 **Why did the 1897 Ottawa Capitals–Montreal Victorias playoff series end abruptly before all the "necessary" games were played?**
A. The Capitals quit because they were outplayed
B. A railway disaster on the eve of the final game
C. The series was too violent
D. The Victorias' home rink burned down

The 1952 semifinals: A hard-fought series that went the distance.

7.11   **Which two players are shaking hands in the photo?**
A. Boston's Tiny Thompson and Montreal's
   Emile Bouchard
B. Boston's Sugar Jim Henry and Montreal's
   Maurice Richard
C. Boston's Frank Brimsek and Montreal's Doug Harvey
D. Boston's Jack Gelineau and Montreal's Elmer Lach

7.12   **How many Stanley Cups were won on Montreal Forum
ice during its 72-year history?**
A. 12 Cups
B. 16 Cups
C. 20 Cups
D. 24 Cups

7.13 Which Montreal player said of Canadiens coach Al MacNeil: "Al MacNeil is the worst coach that I have ever known," during the 1971 Stanley Cup finals?

A. Jean Béliveau
B. Pete Mahovlich
C. John Ferguson
D. Henri Richard

7.14 Why will the Boston Bruins always remember the 1979 semifinals against Montreal?

A. It was the last time Boston made it to the semifinals
B. They lost the seventh game on a bad penalty
C. Coach Don Cherry was ejected from the game for fighting
D. They beat their longtime playoff adversary for the first time

7.15 Which Canadiens player is the only NHLer ever named first, second and third star in a playoff game?

A. Guy Lafleur
B. Yvan Cournoyer
C. Patrick Roy
D. Maurice Richard

7.16 In what Stanley Cup year did the Montreal Canadiens set the professional record for most championships in North American team sports?

A. 1976
B. 1979
C. 1986
D. 1993

7.17 Of the 26 players to win the Stanley Cup six or more times, how many played for the Canadiens?

A. 16 players
B. 20 players
C. 22 players
D. 24 players

Answers

THE BIRTHPLACE OF HOCKEY

7.1 **D. Six teams**

The early years of the Stanley Cup were almost completely dominated by Montreal teams such as the AAA, Victorias and Shamrocks. In fact, during 1907, four of six teams in the east's top league (ECAHA) were from Montreal. Before the Canadiens won their first Cup in 1916, four other Montreal clubs claimed championships of their own. In all, the Stanley Cup has been won 41 times by Montreal teams.

Championship Teams from Montreal		
Cups	Team	Cup-Winning Years
24	Montreal Canadiens	Between 1916 and 1993
5	Montreal Victorias	1895–99
4	Montreal AAA	1893, 94, 1902, 03
4	Montreal Wanderers	1906–08, 10
2	Montreal Shamrocks	1899, 1900
2	Montreal Maroons	1926, 35

7.2 **A. The Ottawa Capitals**

The first Cup challenge match was played at Montreal's Victoria Rink on March 22, 1894, between the AAA and the Capitals. The *Montreal Gazette* reported that the game drew the largest crowd ever packed into the old Montreal rink. "Tin horns, strong lungs and a general rabble predominated." The game was penalty-free, with Montreal winning the match 3–1. Ottawa's Chauncey Kirby scored the first-ever goal in Stanley Cup action. The Cup-winning AAA received gold watches, which cost a total of $190.

7.3   **D. Jean Béliveau**

Although both Richard and Blake have 11 Stanley Cups to Béliveau's 10, it's Big Jean who, after his retirement in 1971, moved upstairs to become the Canadiens' senior vice-president as Montreal won another seven Cups between 1973 and 1993. In all, Béliveau's name appears 17 times on the Stanley Cup. Habs longtime trainer Ed Palchak has been with the team for 10 championships.

7.4   **D. A gold ring**

The championship ring was not always a reward for Cup champions. Gold watches, lapel pins and cash were often customary in early times. One exception came in 1893, the Cup's first year. In compliance with Lord Stanley's terms, the Montreal AAA were awarded the Stanley Cup after winning the AHA title. (No other team dared challenge Montreal, so the Cup was theirs without playing a single playoff game.) As thanks, each player was given a gold ring, a hockey tradition that was only revived by Toronto's dynasty teams of the late 1940s.

7.5   **B. 19 final series games**

During their four-in-a-row championship streak from 1976 to 1979, the Canadiens powerhouse lost only three final games, for a total of 19 games played in four final series. In 1976, Montreal embarrassed the Flyers in four straight; in 1977, they swept Boston, winning game four in overtime; in 1978, Boston came back and managed two victories; and in 1979, the Rangers went down in four straight after taking the first game of the series. Philadelphia's Reggie Leach may have said it best: "The Canadiens have one hell of a hockey team. They've got guys who skate 400 miles an hour and there was no way we could keep up with them." Eight players from that Canadiens team became Hall-of-Famers.

7.6   **B. The Punch Line**

The longest Stanley Cup drought in Montreal history ended the year coach Dick Irvin put Rocket Richard, Toe

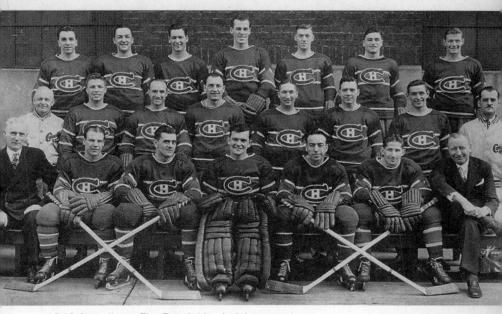

1946 Canadiens: The Punch Line led them to glory.

Blake and Elmer Lach on the same line. They became known as the Punch Line and in 1944 skated rings around Chicago, leading Montreal to its first Cup since 1931. The line's playoff legacy began in game four with the Habs trailing 4–1 in the third period. Spurred on by anger, after Montreal fans booed goalie Bill Durnan, Richard slammed two by Chicago to tie the game 4–4 in regulation time. Then Blake scored the Cup winner at 9:12 of overtime. "It made us so mad," Blake remembers, "that we came from three goals behind to win the Cup in overtime." During that playoff, the Punch Line alone accounted for 21 goals, propelling Montreal from cellar-dwellers to NHL champions.

7.7 **B. He imposed fines and suspended the players himself**
So vicious were the attacks by Montreal defensemen Sprague Cleghorn and Billy Couture in the first game of the 1923 Montreal–Ottawa playoffs that Dandurand didn't even wait for the league to take action; he fined

and suspended his own players. In one incident, after a pretty Ottawa goal by Cy Denneny, Couture clubbed the Senator player as he was returning to take his position for the face-off; later, Cleghorn cross-checked Lionel Hitchman in the face, knocking him out cold. Despite Montreal's rough tactics, Ottawa won the game and eventually the series, leaving Dandurand, a true sportsman, to reflect on his self-imposed suspensions.

7.8

A. The Montreal Maroons

The Forum was just two years old in 1926 when it hosted its first Stanley Cup celebration. The NHL sophomore Maroons challenged the Victoria Cougars, who came east after an exhausting 45-game season and a 3,000-mile train ride. The cross-continent trip was in vain because the Maroons dispatched the Cougars in four games, three by shutouts. The New York Rangers won the next Cup on Forum ice in 1928. It wasn't until 1930 that the Canadiens won their first championship at the Forum, beating Boston in two straight games in the best-of-three finals.

7.9

B. As losers, they refused to shake hands with the winners

White-hot intensity is perhaps the best description for the Red Wings–Canadiens rivalry of the 1950s. Each game, regular or post-season, was a bitter contest between two teams that literally hated each other. Detroit had Gordie Howe, "Terrible" Ted Lindsay and shutout king Terry Sawchuk. Montreal had Rocket Richard, Jean Béliveau and D-man Doug Harvey. Their mutual hatred became legend during 1954's Cup finals in game seven when the two clubs tied 1–1 and headed into overtime. At 4:29 of the extra period, Harvey tried to glove a Tony Leswick shot and instead deflected the puck over Montreal goalie Gerry McNeil's shoulder. To have come so far and lose the Cup on such a bad goal to your worst enemy was too much for Montreal coach Dick Irvin. He led his team off the ice before the customary handshakes, later commenting: "If I had shaken hands, I wouldn't have meant it. I refuse to be a hypocrite."

7.10 **A. The Capitals quit because they were outplayed**

The 1897 best-of-three series was never completed because the Caps were so humiliated after losing the opener to Montreal 14–2 that they never showed up for the second game, sending word to the Victorias that they were abandoning the series "in the best interests of hockey."

7.11 **B. Boston's Sugar Jim Henry and Montreal's Maurice Richard**

Black-eyed, cut up and groggy, Richard scored what many consider the greatest goal of his career during the 1952 semifinals against Boston. It came in game seven, with the score deadlocked 1–1 and four minutes remaining in regulation time. Early in period two, Richard had been knocked unconscious in a heavy collision with the Bruins' Leo Labine. He was helped off the ice and not expected back. But with the game on the line, Richard returned to the ice. Blood dripped down his face. Half-dazed he took a pass from Butch Bouchard and, in a blinding end-to-end rush, swept past the entire Bruins team, wheeled suddenly in front of Boston goalie Jim Henry and whipped a low shot that found the empty corner. The roar from 14,598 fans shook the Forum. The series-winning tally was remembered for years, yet to this day Richard still can't recall his own goal.

7.12 **B. 16 Cups**

In its 72-year history, the Forum has seen four teams celebrate 16 Stanley Cups on its ice. The Canadiens have won 12 of their 24 championships at home; the Montreal Maroons won Cups in 1926 and 1935; the New York Rangers took one Cup in 1928; and the Calgary Flames one Cup in 1989. Calgary is the only NHL team to defeat the Canadiens on Forum ice for the Stanley Cup. New York's Cup victory in 1928 came against the Maroons.

7.13 D. Henri Richard

Over his lengthy playoff career, Richard had many eventful series, but none more dramatic than the 1971 finals against Chicago when he publicly admonished coach Al MacNeil after his game-five benching. The incident turned into a French-English issue, and by the next game MacNeil had plainclothes policemen protecting him behind the bench. Richard apologized and then settled the score his own way. In game seven, down two goals and with the Cup on the line, he brought Montreal back, scoring two goals, including the Stanley Cup winner.

7.14 B. They lost the seventh game on a bad penalty

Any Boston fan over the age of 21 remembers 1979. It was the year the Bruins bumbled the semifinals against Montreal and lost a Stanley Cup that was almost assuredly theirs. In game seven of the semis, with Boston leading 4–3 in the dying moments of regulation time, Boston got a bench penalty for too many men on the ice. On the ensuing power play, as the clock ticked down, the Canadiens' Jacques Lemaire streaked across Boston's blueline and drop-passed the puck to Guy Lafleur. Lafleur, bearing down full-tilt, smoked a 30-footer into the low far corner past a startled Gilles Gilbert. In overtime, Yvon Lambert scored the winner, once more breaking Boston's spirit in the playoffs. The finals were played in anti-climactic fashion, as Montreal easily handled the weaker New York Rangers to win its fourth straight Cup.

7.15 D. Maurice Richard

The only time in NHL history that one player has been named all three game stars occurred on March 23, 1944, after Richard's one-man scoring show during game two of the 1944 Toronto–Montreal semifinals. Richard predicted a big night, boldly telling Maple Leaf goalie Paul Bibeault: "You were too hot for us in game one, Paul. But I'll give you a lot to think about in game two, my friend." True to his word, Richard, in only his second career playoff game, came out storming in an offensive display that blew five goals past his Leaf pal. When Richard was named the third star, the crowd was aghast. Who could have topped the Rocket's five-goal night? Then Richard was selected the second star as well. The Forum crowd immediately caught on, cheering in anticipation of the next announcement. It turned into pure theatre as another loud roar engulfed the Forum in approval of Richard's first-star selection. The Canadiens never looked back after that 5–1 win. They pummelled Toronto and then Chicago, racking up seven consecutive victories to win the Stanley Cup.

7.16 **C. 1986**
The Canadiens established the professional record for team championships in 1986 by defeating the Calgary Flames to win their 23rd Stanley Cup. Baseball's New York Yankees have amassed 22 World Series titles.

7.17 **B. 20 players**
Among the 1,700 champions inscribed on the Stanley Cup, there are an impressive number of Canadiens, many of whom have multiple championships. A remarkable 20 of 26 NHLers with six or more Cups are Montreal players, including Henri Richard with 11 Cups; Jean Béliveau, Yvan Cournoyer (10); Claude Provost (nine); Jacques Lemaire, Maurice Richard (eight); Serge Savard, Jean-Guy Talbot (seven). The six-time winners include Ralph Backstrom, Ken Dryden, Bernie Geoffrion, Doug Harvey, Tom Johnson, Jacques Laperrière, Guy Lapointe, Dickie Moore, Jacques Plante and Larry Robinson. Dick Duff and Frank Mahovlich won six Cups as members of both the Canadiens and Toronto Maple Leafs. The non-Canadiens Cup winners who have won six or more are Jack Marshall, Red Kelly, Bryan Trottier, Mark Messier, Kevin Lowe and Glenn Anderson.

RECORDS OF THE CUP FINALS

The players listed below each hold a record in Stanley Cup final series play. Match the 18 NHLers with their records. To help you, each record provides some clues of the true record holder.

(Solutions are on page 138)

Bobby Orr   Toe Blake   Paul Coffey   Larry Murphy
Brian Skrudland Jaromir Jagr   Ken Dryden   Jean Béliveau
Maurice Richard Roy Conacher   Jacques Plante   Mike Bossy
Tony Esposito   Wayne Gretzky   Mel Bridgman   Gordie Howe
Bernie Geoffrion Yvan Cournoyer

1. _____ holds the record for playing in 53 consecutive final series games between 1951 and 1960. (It's not Gordie Howe.)

2. _____ scored at 0:09 seconds of overtime on May 18, 1986, to establish the record for the fastest goal from the start of a period in the finals.

3. _____ set the record for most career goals in the finals by scoring 34 goals in 59 games, a record that tops teammate Jean Béliveau's by four goals.

4. _____ gave up 33 goals in six games during the 1973 finals against Montreal to set the record for most goals allowed by a netminder in a final series.

5. _____ amassed 94 minutes in box time over his lengthy career to establish the record for most career penalty minutes in the finals.

6. _____ shares the record for most points by a defenseman in one final series with Brian Leetch. While Leetch scored his 11 points in seven games, our man did it in five.

7. _____ scored five goals in 1939 and still holds the record for most goals by a rookie in a final series. His team won the Cup that year.

8. _____ sets the record for most goals in a six-game final series, scoring six times in 1973's Cup final.

9. _____ recorded 10 straight final series victories between 1976 and 1978 to become the record holder for the most consecutive wins by a goalie in the finals.

10. _____ set the record for most assists by a defenseman in one final series by chalking up nine assists in six games for Pittsburgh in 1991.

11. _____ made five assists in six games for Pittsburgh during the 1991 finals, setting the record for most assists by a rookie in one Cup final.

12. _____ of the Philadelphia Flyers was assessed 53 minutes in box time during six games in 1980. He still holds the record for most penalty minutes in one final series.

13. _____ tops Jean Béliveau and Gordie Howe (who each have 32 assists) with a record 35 assists in 31 games and holds the record for most career assists in the finals.

14. _____ scored seven goals in 1982's finals to set the record for most goals in a four-game final series.

15. _____ holds the record for most Stanley Cup champion-ships won by a coach. He has eight Cups.

16. _____ scored two points in 1970, one point in 1972 and another point in 1974 to set a record of four points for most career shorthanded points in finals action.

17. _____ still holds the record for most career wins by a goalie in the finals with 25.

18. _____ notched 62 points in 64 games to set the mark for most career points in the finals, a record nine points better than Wayne Gretzky's total in this category.

Chapter EIGHT

THE HOT PLAYOFF GOALIE

When Detroit goalie Norm Smith was sidelined with an elbow injury during game one of the 1937 finals, the Wings called up veteran minor leaguer Earl Robertson of the International League's Pittsburgh Hornets to complete the series. After losing his NHL debut 5–1 to New York, Robertson won three of four matches for Detroit, including two shutouts in the finals' last two games, to win the Cup. In this chapter, we champion the hot playoff goaltender, who can break the opposition's spirit more effectively than any other player on the ice.

(Answers are on page 110)

8.1 **As of 1996, which goalie holds the playoff record for most games played?**
A. Billy Smith
B. Glenn Hall
C. Grant Fuhr
D. Patrick Roy

8.2 **What new piece of equipment did Winnipeg Victorias goalie George Merritt use during the 1895 finals?**
A. A military-issue helmet
B. The first "wide-bodied" goalie stick
C. Cricket pads strapped to his legs
D. Goalie skates

8.3 **In 1931, Bruins coach Art Ross tried what newspapers of the day called, "an amazing manoeuvre" with goalie Tiny Thompson. It was an NHL first. What was Ross's "manoeuvre?"**

A. He forced Thompson to serve his own penalty

B. He invented goalie skates for Thompson

C. He pulled Thompson to add an extra forward

D. He taught Thompson to shoot the puck into the neutral zone

8.4 **Who wore the first goalie face mask in Stanley Cup action, and what was the year?**

A. Clint Benedict, 1929

B. Turk Broda, 1952

C. Glenn Hall, 1956

D. Jacques Plante, 1960

8.5 **How many goalies have registered three shutouts in one best-of-seven playoff series?**

A. Five goalies

B. 10 goalies

C. 15 goalies

D. 20 goalies

8.6 **Who was the oldest goalie to see Stanley Cup action?**

A. Johnny Bower

B. Lester Patrick

C. Jacques Plante

D. Gump Worsley

8.7 **What is unique about Chicago goalie Charlie Gardiner's 1934 inscription on the Stanley Cup?**

A. Next to his name was stamped "Coach"

B. His name was stamped upside down

C. His name was stamped twice

D. Next to his name was stamped "Capt."

8.8 **What is the most number of shutouts recorded in a best-of-seven Stanley Cup finals?**
A. Three shutouts
B. Four shutouts
C. Five shutouts
D. Six shutouts

8.9 **Lester Patrick was an outstanding defenseman, coach and manager. What did he do related to goaltending?**
A. Invented the B-shaped goalie net
B. Occasionally tended goal
C. Promoted the use of goalie masks
D. Stitched up injured goalies

8.10 **Which goalie was the first player on a *losing* team to win the Conn Smythe Trophy as playoff MVP?**
A. Roger Crozier
B. Ron Hextall
C. Bernie Parent
D. Glenn Hall

8.11 **Goalie Harry "Hap" Holmes won how many Cups on how many different teams?**
A. Two Cups on three different teams
B. Three Cups on two different teams
C. Three Cups on three different teams
D. Four Cups on three different teams

8.12 **What caused the backroom brawl at the beginning of the 1938 finals between the Leafs and the Hawks?**
A. An ongoing feud between opposing goalies
B. The selection of a substitute goalie for the Hawks
C. A dispute over a playoff suspension to a goalie
D. The use of a referee whose brother was the Leafs' goalie

8.13 **Why is Boston goalie Hal Winkler's name on the Stanley Cup as part of the Bruins' victorious 1929 team, even though he retired in 1928?**

A. He was the Bruins' manager in 1929

B. Boston wanted to honour him

C. The Cup engraver added Winkler's name by mistake

D. He came out of retirement to play one game in the 1929 finals

8.14 **What is the longest time one goalie has blanked the opposition in Stanley Cup action?**

A. Less than 120 minutes of play

B. Between 120 and 180 minutes of play

C. Between 180 and 240 minutes of play

D. More than 240 minutes of play

8.15 **Which two opposing goalie greats, who won multiple Stanley Cups and Vezina Trophies during the 1940s, died within two weeks of each other?**

A. Turk Broda and Terry Sawchuck

B. Bill Durnan and Johnny Bower

C. Jacques Plante and Al Rollins

D. Bill Durnan and Turk Broda

8.16 **As of 1996, how many goalies in NHL history have 60 or more playoff wins?**

A. Six goalies

B. 12 goalies

C. 18 goalies

D. 24 goalies

THE HOT PLAYOFF GOALIE

8.1 **D. Patrick Roy**
During the 1996 playoffs, Roy overtook Smith's 132 play-off-game record, netminding in 22 post-season matches to win his third Stanley Cup. Barring injuries, Grant Fuhr is next in line to overtake the 17-year Islander veteran.

Most Playoff Games by Goalies

Games	Player	Min.	GA	SO	GAA	Cups
136	Patrick Roy	8,418	336	8	2.38	3
132	Billy Smith	7,645	348	5	2.73	4
121	Grant Fuhr	7,071	358	3	3.06	5
116	Andy Moog	6,529	332	3	3.05	3
115	Glenn Hall	6,899	321	6	2.79	1
112	Jacques Plante	6,651	241	14	2.17	6
112	Ken Dryden	6,846	274	10	2.40	6

8.2 **C. Cricket pads strapped to his legs**
In an era when players used almost no protective equipment, it must have been quite the spectacle to witness George Merritt skate onto the ice wearing white cricket pads. His innovation set the standard for all future goalies, particularly since Merritt recorded history's first Stanley Cup shutout during the game, a 2–0 win over the Montreal Victorias.

8.3 **C. He pulled Thompson to add an extra forward**
Ross was the first coach to yank his goalie for an extra attacker. In the 1931 Montreal–Boston semifinals, with one loss already and behind 1–0 in game two, Ross gam-

bled in the dying moments and pulled Tiny Thompson to add a forward. The scheme didn't work; Boston still lost to Montreal 1–0. But what the day's sports pages called an "amazing manoeuvre" caught on and soon became standard game strategy.

8.4   D. Jacques Plante, 1960

Although the Maroons' Clint Benedict was the first goalie to use face protection in an NHL game, Plante was the first to regularly don a mask and the first to do so during playoff action. Three decades after Benedict tried his crude leather mask in 1930, Plante engineered a mask of plastic and, despite much opposition from coach Toe Blake, wore it through most of 1959–60. To prove Blake and other critics of the goalie mask wrong, Plante had to play especially well. And he did, capturing the Vezina Trophy as best goalie that year. Furthermore, the Canadiens took the Stanley Cup undefeated, winning eight straight playoff games, backstopped by Plante's eye-popping 1.38 goals-against average.

8.5   A. Five goalies

Since 1939, only five netminders in NHL history have posted three shutouts in one post-season series. The first was New York's Davey Kerr in 1940's semifinals against Boston. Then, three Toronto goalies did it: Frank McCool in the 1945 Toronto–Detroit finals, Turk Broda in 1950's semis against Detroit and Felix Potvin in 1994's quarterfinals win over Chicago. New Jersey's Martin Brodeur became just the fifth goaltender to record three SOs in a playoff round, a 1995 quarterfinals win against Boston.

8.6   A. Johnny Bower

Bower's last playoff game was on April 6, 1969, his 74th career match. He was 44 years, four months and 28 days old. Right behind him are Lester Patrick, who, as Rangers manager, backstopped one game during the 1928 playoffs at the age of 44 years, three months and eight days. Plante ended his NHL playoff career in 1973 with Boston at the age of 44 years, two months and 19 days. Worsley was the youngster at the age of 42 years, 10 months and 28 days.

8.7   **D. Next to his name was stamped "Capt."**
Gardiner made the most of a very short hockey career. During his brief seven-year stint backstopping the Blackhawks, Gardiner won two Vezina Trophies as top netminder, was named to the All-Star team four times, recorded 42 shutouts, a career 2.02 GAA and a phenomenal 1.37 GAA during post-season play. His widespread respect earned him the Hawks captaincy in 1933–34, the season they won the Stanley Cup. Gardiner's playoff performance was a remarkable achievement. He had been unable to beat a bout of tonsillitis, which over the months had spread to his kidneys. By playoff time, he was racked with pain, often blacking out before a game. But he still managed a 1.50 playoff GAA. Two months after the championship season, Charlie Gardiner died at his Winnipeg home from a brain hemorrhage. He was inducted into the Hockey Hall of Fame in 1945. Today, he remains the only goalie to captain a Stanley Cup winner.

8.8   **C. Five shutouts**
The 1945 playoffs were one of the greatest post-seasons in NHL history. The three best-of-seven series (two semifinals and one final) took 20 games to complete (just one game less than the maximum 21). In the first match-up, the third-place Leafs surprised the defending Cup-champion Canadiens in six games. The other semifinal series went to Detroit after a hard-fought seven-game battle against Boston. Then, for the first time in NHL history, two rookie netminders, Toronto's Frank McCool and Detroit's Harry Lumley, faced each other in the finals. Rookie McCool posted three straight shutouts, 1–0, 2–0 and 1–0, to set a Stanley Cup record. In game four, Detroit rebounded 5–3 to stave off elimination. Lumley followed with his own rookie shutout streak, blanking the Leafs 2–0 and 1–0 in games five and six. Five

Chicago's Charlie Gardiner:
The NHL's only Stanley
Cup-winning goalie captain.

Lester Patrick: The 44-year-old coach who subbed in nets and became 1928's Stanley Cup hero.

SOs in six final series games by two rookie netminders! In game seven at Detroit's Olympia, Toronto, a third-place team that had finished 28 points back of the regular-season leaders, edged Detroit 2–1 to win the Cup. For McCool, the Cup-winning rookie, those 13 post-season games in 1945 were the only ones of his career. Lumley's NHL career took a different turn. A 76 playoff-game veteran and Cup winner with Detroit in 1950, he back-stopped until 1960.

8.9   B. Occasionally tended goal

As a player, coach and manager, Lester Patrick made four recorded appearances in the net. Playing point man for the Brandon Wheat Kings in 1904, he replaced goalie Don Morrison during a penalty. While managing the Victoria Cougars in 1922, he took over Norm Fowler's crease for a full 10 minutes, stopping a penalty shot from Jack Adams. Two nights later, he did it again when Fowler was benched for fighting. But his most famous foray between the pipes came at age 44 while serving as the New York Rangers' coach/manager during the 1928 Cup finals versus the Montreal Maroons. In the second game, goalie Lorne Chabot caught the puck square in the left eye and had to be taken to the hospital. With no spare, Patrick asked to use either Alex Connell or Hughie McCormick, both of whom were in the stands. Maroons coach Eddie Gerard refused, so Patrick put on Chabot's blood-stained pads and stepped into the crease. He allowed only one goal in the Rangers' 2–1 overtime win.

8.10   A. Roger Crozier

Although Detroit lost the 1966 Cup finals to Montreal, Crozier had a sensational playoff series. Finishing the regular season in fourth place and 16 points behind the league-leading Canadiens, Detroit was hardly favoured. But the Wings surprised everyone by stealing two wins in Montreal on Crozier's brilliant netminding. Games three and four went to the fired-up Canadiens, with Detroit just holding its own after Crozier suffered a twisted ankle in a goal-crease crash with Bobby Rousseau. Crozier returned for the fifth game, but his injury was too much and the Wings lost 5–1. In game six, Detroit rebounded to outshoot the Habs 30–22 in a 2–2 tie after regulation time. In overtime, a controversial goal handed Montreal the Cup. As Henri Richard slid towards the net, he somehow redirected the puck past Crozier for the series winner. The Wings were finished, but Crozier walked away with the Conn Smythe as playoff MVP, posting a 2.17 goals-against average and one shutout in 12 games. He was both the first member of a losing team and the first netminder to win MVP playoff honours.

8.11 **D. Four Cups on three different teams**
Holmes was a "right place-right time" kind of goalie when it came to the Stanley Cup: four Cups on three different teams. In 1914, his second year of pro hockey, he helped the Toronto Blueshirts win the NHA championship and the Cup in a two-game, total-goals series against the Canadiens. In 1917, he celebrated with the Seattle Metropolitans, who defeated Montreal three games to one to become the first American team to officially win the Cup. In 1918, the NHL's inaugural season, he brought his Cup-luck to the Toronto Blueshirts (a.k.a. the Arenas) again. And finally, Holmes was in the net for the Victoria Cougars' victory in 1925, the last time a non-NHL team captured the Cup.

8.12 **B. The selection of a substitute goalie for the Hawks**
When the Blackhawks arrived in Toronto for the 1938 finals, their first job was to find a backup for injured netminder Mike Karakas. Coach Bill Stewart asked to use Ranger great Davey Kerr but the Leafs refused, suggesting instead Alfie Moore, an ex-New York American backstopper who was in Toronto. Thinking he was being helpful, Toronto's Frank Selke called up Moore and suggested he come over to the Gardens. Even as fans arrived for the first game, the issue wasn't settled. When Stewart found out that Selke had called up Moore, he accused

Selke of trying to pawn off a half-sober goaltender on his team. Leaf GM Conn Smythe, also at the scene, yelled, "Nobody calls Selke a liar in my presence," and attacked Stewart. After the fracas was settled, Moore stepped between the pipes for the Hawks, doing an excellent job in a 3–1 Chicago victory. Moore later admitted, "Sure I had a few beers. But I had no idea I was going to play that night."

8.13   **B. Boston wanted to honour him**
Winkler didn't play pro hockey until age 30 when he back-stopped the WCHL Edmonton Eskimos in 1922. After the western-based league folded in 1926, Winkler landed in New York and Boston, playing almost two years for the Bruins before retiring at 36. Winkler's last season was his best: he led the NHL in minutes played (2,780) and tied the great Alex Connell for most shutouts (15). With a sparkling 1.59 GAA, Winkler left the game on top. Or so he thought. In his retirement year, the Bruins, with rookie goalie Tiny Thompson, led the American Division and then beat the Rangers for the coveted Stanley Cup. Boston felt Winkler deserved some credit so they included him in the team's championship picture and added his name on the Cup: "Hal Winkler, sub-goaltender."

8.14   **D. More than 240 minutes of play**
Norm Smith may not be remembered today, but in 1936 no one could stop talking about his 248 minute 32 second shutout sequence during the Red Wings–Maroons semi-final series. Smith's record began on March 24 in game one as Detroit battled Montreal through three regulation periods and until 16:30 of the *sixth* overtime period, when the Red Wings' Mud Bruneteau scored on Maroon goalie Lorne Chabot. The 176:30 minutes of play marked the longest game in playoff history. Smith continued his streak through three more periods of game two, zeroing Montreal 3–0. Finally, at 12:02 of game three, Gus Marker scored on Smith, stopping the clock on his record: 248 minutes and 32 seconds of shutout hockey. It's a playoff record that may never be broken.

Bill Durnan and Turk Broda: The game's two best goalies of the 1940s.

8.15   **D. Bill Durnan and Turk Broda**

One of hockey's greatest old-time rivalries was the Toronto-Montreal ice feuds of the 1940s. The intensity was due, in no small measure, to Broda and Durnan, arguably the two best goalies of the era. While Broda won the Stanley Cup five times, Durnan dominated individual awards. In his seven NHL seasons, Durnan won the Vezina Trophy as top goalie six times and was named to six First All-Star Teams. As brothers-in-arms in the goaltending trade, they dominated the game, each managing consecutive seasons of silverware, only broken by the other. Broda and Durnan won everything. Curiously, both died within weeks of each other in October 1972.

8.16   **A. Six goalies**

Only six netminders in NHL history have recorded 60-plus wins in playoff action. As we move towards the year 2000, both Patrick Roy and Grant Fuhr are challenging leader Billy Smith in this category. Tom Barrasso should become the next goalie with more than 60 wins.

Most Career Playoff Wins

Goalie	GP	W	L	SO	GAA	Cups
Billy Smith	132	88	36	5	2.73	4
Patrick Roy	136	86	48	8	2.38	3
Ken Dryden	112	80	32	10	2.40	6
Grant Fuhr	121	78	36	3	3.06	5
Jacques Plante	112	71	37	14	2.17	6
Andy Moog	116	61	48	3	3.05	3
Turk Broda	101	58	42	13	1.98	5
Tom Barrasso	94	51	39	5	3.15	2

THE PLAYOFF MVP

Before the Stanley Cup is presented on the ice to the winning team, the Conn Smythe Trophy is awarded to the playoffs' most valuable player. It doesn't always go to top scorers, but often to defensive specialists and sometimes even to a member of the Cup-losing contingent. Match the MVPs below and the championship season in which they won their Conn Smythe.   *(Solutions are on page 139*

Dave Keon	Joe Sakic	Roger Crozier	Wayne Gretzky
Mike Bossy	Bobby Orr	Patrick Roy	Butch Goring
Ken Dryden	Bill Ranford	Reggie Leach	Claude Lemieux
Bernie Parent	Mario Lemieux	Ron Hextall	Bob Gainey
Jean Béliveau	Al McInnis	Glenn Hall	Brian Leetch

1. _____ 1965 Chicago vs. Montreal
2. _____ 1966 Montreal vs. Detroit
3. _____ 1967 Toronto vs. Montreal
4. _____ 1968 St.Louis vs. Montreal
5. _____ 1971 Montreal vs. Boston
6. _____ 1972 Boston vs. NYR
7. _____ 1975 Philadelphia vs. Buffalo
8. _____ 1976 Montreal vs. Philadelphia
9. _____ 1979 NYR vs. Montreal
10. _____ 1981 Minnesota vs. NYI
11. _____ 1982 NYI vs. Vancouver
12. _____ 1985 Edmonton vs. Philadelphia
13. _____ 1987 Philadelphia vs. Edmonton
14. _____ 1989 Calgary vs. Montreal
15. _____ 1990 Edmonton vs. Boston
16. _____ 1991 Pittsburgh vs. Minnesota
17. _____ 1993 Montreal vs. Los Angeles
18. _____ 1994 Vancouver vs. NYR
19. _____ 1995 Detroit vs. New Jersey
20. _____ 1996 Colorado vs. Florida

THE BIG DANCE

What are the odds of a team capturing the Stanley Cup after winning the first game of the finals? Or after taking both of the first two games? The percentages are excellent. The following trends have evolved: teams winning game one took the Cup 45 of 56 times (80 per cent); teams winning both games one and two claimed the Cup 34 of 37 times (92 per cent); teams holding a 2–1 series lead won the Cup 30 of 35 times (86 per cent); and teams holding a 3–2 series lead took the Cup 21 of 25 times or 84 per cent. In this chapter, we go to the big dance, the Stanley Cup finals, to test your own winning percentage.

(Answers are on page 125)

9.1 **Which team boasted a 35-game undefeated streak during the 1979–80 regular season, propelling it to the Cup finals that year?**
A. The Montreal Canadiens
B. The Pittsburgh Penguins
C. The New York Islanders
D. The Philadelphia Flyers

9.2 **Which modern-day team took the least time to reach the Cup finals after entering the NHL?**
A. The Buffalo Sabres
B. The Edmonton Oilers
C. The St. Louis Blues
D. The Florida Panthers

9.3 **Why were the 1919 finals never completed?**
A. A flu epidemic sidelined many of the players
B. The series was reportedly fixed
C. Both coaches were fired for fighting
D. The host arena experienced ice problems

9.4 **Why were the New York Rangers forced to play every game of the 1950 Stanley Cup final series on the road?**
A. The circus was using Madison Square Garden
B. Madison Square Garden was under renovation
C. Not enough tickets were sold in New York
D. Because the club couldn't pay its rent

9.5 **What is the greatest number of career overtime goals one player has scored in the Stanley Cup finals?**
A. No one has scored more than one OT goal in the finals
B. Two OT goals
C. Three OT goals
D. Four OT goals

9.6 **What is the greatest number of years any one NHLer has played in the Stanley Cup finals?**
A. Four years
B. Eight years
C. 12 years
D. 16 years

9.7 **How many all-Canadian final series have there been since Toronto met Montreal in 1967?**
A. None
B. One all-Canadian final series
C. Two all-Canadian final series
D. Four all-Canadian final series

9.8 **Who is the youngest player to win the Conn Smythe trophy?**

A. Wayne Gretzky

B. Bryan Trottier

C. Patrick Roy

D. Bobby Orr

9.9 **What made the 1951 finals between the Leafs and the Canadiens a real "heart-stopper" of a series?**

A. Every game went into overtime

B. Every game ended with a brawl

C. Every game had a penalty shot

D. Every game ended with the goalie pulled for an extra man

9.10 **What is the fewest number of games by which one NHL team has won the championship in the Stanley Cup finals?**

A. One final series game

B. Two final series games

C. Three final series games

D. Four final series games

9.11 **Since 1927, how many Stanley Cup-winning goals have been scored in overtime?**

A. Two goals

B. Seven goals

C. 13 goals

D. 18 goals

9.12 **Which NHL dynasty boasts the top five players in the "most consecutive games played in the finals" category?**

A. The 1950s Detroit Red Wings

B. The 1980s Edmonton Oilers

C. The 1950s Montreal Canadiens

D. The 1980s New York Islanders

9.13 **In Stanley Cup final series action, what playoff game had the most penalties by two teams?**
A. Game five of the 1974 Philadelphia–Boston finals
B. Game five of the 1978 Montreal–Boston finals
C. Game six of the 1980 New York–Philadelphia finals
D. Game four of the 1986 Montreal–Calgary finals

9.14 **What is the most penalty minutes amassed by two teams during a Stanley Cup final series?**
A. 211 minutes
B. 311 minutes
C. 411 minutes
D. 511 minutes

9.15 **What did the Philadelphia Flyers do to try to psyche out the Bruins during game six of the 1974 finals?**
A. They wore new playoff jerseys
B. They painted the Stanley Cup on the ice at the Spectrum
C. They hired a famous singer to belt out "God Bless America"
D. They handed out white pom-poms to the spectators

9.16 **Since the Conn Smythe Trophy was first awarded in 1965, how many players have won it twice? Name the player(s).**
A. One player
B. Three players
C. Five players
D. Seven players

9.17 **Seven penalty shots have been awarded in the Stanley Cup finals. How many have made it into the net?**
A. None
B. Two
C. Four
D. Six

9.1   **D. The Philadelphia Flyers**

Philadelphia's record unbeaten streak of 25 wins and 10 ties in 1979–80 launched the team into the playoffs with a league-leading 116 points and a 48–12–20 record. That momentum continued with just two losses in three playoff rounds against Edmonton, the Rangers and Minnesota. But in the finals, it was a different story. The Islanders, led by Mike Bossy, Bryan Trottier and Billy Smith, took game one 4–3 on a Denis Potvin power play goal in overtime. The next four games were one-sided victories, split between two talented teams, each looking to make its mark in Stanley Cup history. The Islanders were playing for their first championship; the Flyers to top off a stellar season. Game six went into overtime tied 4–4. At 7:11 of overtime, Islander John Tonelli passed the puck to Bobby Nystrom, who redirected it past Flyers goaltender Pete Peeters. For Philadelphia, there was little solace after coming so far with so many regular-season victories.

9.2   **C. The St. Louis Blues**

Circumstances play a big role in determining this winner. When expansion doubled the NHL and it went from six to 12 teams in 1967, the league assigned the new clubs to one division, guaranteeing an expansion city a shot at the Stanley Cup. St. Louis was the eventual winner in the western playoff rounds leading up to the finals. Of course, the Blues got blown out 4–0 by the long-established Canadiens. For the three-year-old 1996 Stanley Cup finalist Florida Panthers, circumstances also worked to their advantage when favourable rules in the 1993 expansion draft enabled them to acquire veterans such as John Vanbiesbrouck and Brian Skrudland.

Least Number of Years for New Team to Reach Finals

Years	Team	1st Season	1st Final	Outcome
1	St. Louis	1967	1968	4–0 loss to Montreal
3	Florida	1993	1996	4–0 loss to Colorado
4	Edmonton	1979	1983	4–0 loss to NY Islanders
5	Buffalo	1970	1975	4–2 loss to Philadelphia
7	Philadelphia	1967	1974	4–2 win over Boston
8	NY Islanders	1972	1980	4–2 win over Philadelphia

9.3 **A. A flu epidemic sidelined many of the players**

In more than 100 years of hockey, only one season, 1919, failed to produce a Stanley Cup champion. After five games Seattle and Montreal were deadlocked, each team with two wins and a tie. In game five, though, something was very wrong. Fans could see that the players were fatigued and dragging themselves around the ice. At one point, Montreal forward Joe Hall collapsed with a high fever. The next day, players were hospitalized and the sixth match cancelled just hours before game time. The influenza epidemic had hit hockey and with it came tragedy: Joe Hall died five days later in Seattle from pneumonia brought on by the flu. The 1919 series was cancelled.

9.4 **A. The circus was using Madison Square Garden**

Logistical conflicts between Barnum & Bailey's circus and the Stanley Cup finals have a rich tradition at Madison Square Garden. Ever since the 1920s, if "the biggest show on earth" was at MSG, the Rangers were forced to play their home games on the road at a neutral or "away-home" site. In 1928, New York played the entire finals against the Maroons at the Montreal Forum. They won the Cup that year, but most other playoff seasons were more demanding. In 1950, the Rangers spent the entire time riding trains between Detroit's

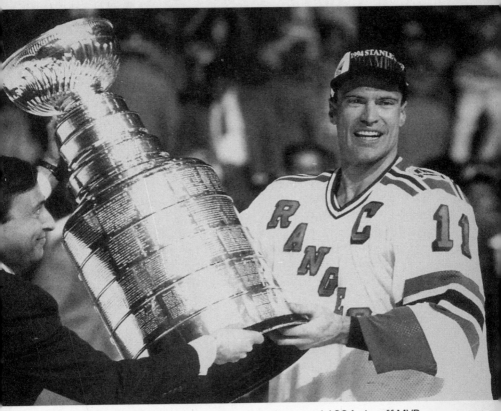

Ranger captain Mark Messier: six-time Cup-winner and 1994 playoff MVP.

Olympia and their "away-home" of Maple Leaf Gardens in Toronto. Going into game six the Rangers were on a roll, ahead 3–2 in the series. But the next game, scheduled for Toronto, was moved to Detroit because an NHL rule required that a deciding Stanley Cup game could not be played at a neutral site. So in game six, Detroit became the home site for the visiting Rangers! And since game seven was also a deciding Cup game, it too was played at the Olympia. In all, five games were played in Detroit and just two in Toronto (and obviously none in New York). In game seven, in double overtime, the Red Wings prevailed before a wild hometown crowd. The Rangers were crushed. A New York hockey crowd under similar circumstances may have helped the boys in blue. Today, things are different: MSG can accommodate both the circus and hockey. While the 1996 playoff games roared on, not 50 feet from the penalty box the backstage area was filled with elephants, lions and trapeze equipment.

9.5 ### C. Three OT goals

Between 1939 and 1996, 50 games have gone into overtime in finals Cup action. In those contests, only four players have scored more than one overtime final series goal. Montreal's Jacques Lemaire pegged one in 1968 and another in 1977. Don Raleigh of the Rangers scored two in consecutive games in 1950 and the Canadiens' John LeClair did it in 1993, the only two NHLers to post back-to-back overtime finals goals. The fourth player, Maurice Richard, holds the record with three overtime goals scored in the 1946, 1951 and 1958 finals.

9.6 ### C. 12 years

Remarkably, not one but four players have reached the finals 12 times, an NHL record. Three of the four are Montreal Canadiens, two come from the same family (the Richards) and one (Red Kelly) did it with two different teams. A number of other prominent names, such as Doug Harvey (11) and Gordie Howe (10), also have double-digit final appearances. Yvan Cournoyer's 10 final series were special. He won the Stanley Cup every time.

Most Years in Stanley Cup Finals

Years	Player	Team	Final Appearances	Cups
12	M. Richard	Montreal	1944, 46, 47, 51–60	8
12	R. Kelly	Detroit, Toronto	1948, 49, 50, 52, 54–56, 60, 62–64, 67	8
12	J. Béliveau	Montreal	1954–60, 1965–69, 71	10
12	H. Richard	Montreal	1956–60, 65–69, 71, 73	11

9.7　**C. Two all-Canadian final series**
Since the Canadiens and Maple Leafs clashed in 1967's classic final series, only two other all-Canadian finals have occurred, both between Montreal and Calgary. Each team won a Cup, the Canadiens in 1986 and the Flames in 1989.

9.8　**C. Patrick Roy**
Roy was just 20 years old and an NHL rookie when he won the Conn Smythe in 1986. The former Canadiens netminder posted a record-tying 15 wins and a 1.92 GAA in 20 post-season games. Orr was 22 during his MVP playoff season in 1970. Who is the oldest playoff MVP? Goalie Glenn Hall, who, at age 37, won MVP honours for St. Louis in 1968.

9.9　**A. Every game went into overtime**
Even though the 1951 Toronto–Montreal best-of-seven Stanley Cup finals ended in just five games, every match was a thriller, requiring sudden-death overtime to settle each outcome. But all the overtimes ended quickly, in under six minutes, with the Maple Leafs summarily dispatching the Canadiens in all but game two. If there was a series star, it would have to be Toronto's Bill Barilko. During game one, he drove headfirst into the Leafs' open net to stop Rocket Richard's slap shot and preserve a 2–2 score in regulation time. In the series' final game, he whipped the puck past Montreal goalie Gerry McNeil for the overtime Cup winner.

The 1951 Stanley Cup Finals

Game	Final Score	OT Scorer	OT Time
1	Tor 3–Mtl 2	Sid Smith	5:51
2	Mtl 3–Tor 2	Rocket Richard	2:55
3	Tor 2–Mtl 1	Ted Kennedy	4:47
4	Tor 3–Mtl 2	Harry Watson	5:15
5	Tor 3–Mtl 2	Bill Barilko	2:53

9.10 **B. Two final series games**

Since the NHL assumed control of Stanley Cup competition in 1926, only two teams—the 1929 Boston Bruins and 1930 Montreal Canadiens—have captured the Cup in the fewest possible games, two straight in the best-of-three finals format. The next quickest winners are the 1932 Toronto Maple Leafs and 1935 Montreal Maroons, both of whom won the Cup in three straight games in their best-of-five series. Since the seven-game format began in 1939, 17 finals have ended in 4–0 sweeps.

9.11 **C. 13 goals**

Between 1927 and 1996, 13 players have potted Cup winners in overtime (11 Cup winners were in best-of-seven series and two in best-of-five series). In the five-game series (1933, 1934), both overtime goals were netted in the fourth game. In the seven-game series, four overtime Cup winners were scored in game four, two in game five and three in game six. Two Stanley Cup-winning goals were scored in overtime in the seventh and deciding game, both by Detroit, in 1950 and 1954.

Stanley Cup-Winning Goals in Overtime

Year	Player	Team	Time	Score	Series	Losing Goalie
1933	Bill Cook	NYR	7:34	1–0	3–1	Lorne Chabot
1934	Mush March	Chi	30:05	1–0	3–1	Wilfrid Cude
1940	Bryan Hextall	NYR	2:07	3–2	4–2	Turk Broda
1944	Toe Blake	Mtl	9:12	5–4	4–0	Mike Karakas
1950	Pete Babando	Det	28:31	4–3	4–3	Chuck Rayner
1951	Bill Barilko	Tor	2:53	3–2	4–1	Gerry McNeil
1953	Elmer Lach	Mtl	1.22	1–0	4–1	Jim Henry
1954	Tony Leswick	Det	4:20	2–1	4–3	Gerry McNeil
1966	Henri Richard	Mtl	2:20	3–2	4–2	Roger Crozier
1970	Bobby Orr	Bos	0:40	4–3	4–0	Glenn Hall
1977	J. Lemaire	Mtl	4:32	2–1	4–0	Gerry Cheevers
1980	Bob Nystrom	NYI	7:11	5–4	4–2	Pete Peeters
1996	Uwe Krupp	Col	44:31	1–0	4–0	J. Vanbiesbrouck

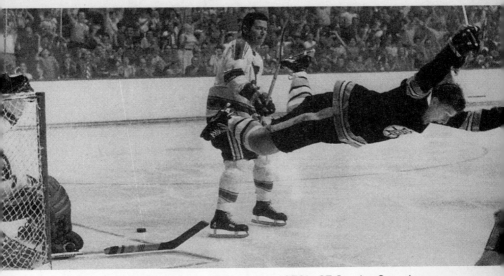

Bobby Orr's midair celebration after scoring 1970's OT Stanley Cup winner.

9.12 **C. The 1950s Montreal Canadiens**

No Cup contender can compare to Montreal's dominance of the 1950s. The Canadiens reached the finals an incredible 10 years in a row, playing 53 final games and capturing six Cups. It's no wonder six Canadiens from those teams top the NHL list for most consecutive games played in the finals. As Montreal roared through 53 final games from April 11, 1951, to April 14, 1960, only one Hab played in every match: Bernie "Boom-Boom" Geoffrion.

Most Consecutive Final Games

Games	Player	Length of Streak
53	Bernie Geoffrion	Game 1/1951 to Game 4/1960
48	Dickie Moore	Game 1/1952 to Game 4/1960
41	Floyd Curry	Game 1/1951 to Game 3/1958
40	Bert Olmstead	Game 1/1951 to Game 2/1958
38	Tom Johnson	Game 1/1951 to Game 5/1957
36	Doug Harvey	Game 1/1954 to Game 4/1960

9.13 **A. Game five of the 1974 Philadelphia–Boston finals**

It's to be expected that any 1970s playoff match-up between the Flyers and Bruins would spark a few NHL records in box time, especially in Cup finals action. In game five, with the Big Bad Bruins down 3–1 in games to the Broad Street Bullies, no-holds-barred hockey brought out the worst in the two clubs. A record 43 penalties were called in a procession of fights, high-stickings, spearings and butt-ending penalties. Boston won the May 16 melee 5–1, but crashed in game six at the Philadelphia Spectrum, losing the Cup by a 1–0 decision to the Flyers. The six-game series produced a total of 142 penalties by both teams, an NHL record.

9.14 **D. 511 minutes**

Calgary and Montreal duelled in 1986's five-game finals, accumulating a record 511 penalty minutes, split almost evenly between the Flames (256 minutes) and the Canadiens (255 minutes). Although the series is best remembered for rookie standouts Patrick Roy and Claude Lemieux and the fastest goal in overtime playoff action (by Brian Skrudland), a total of six NHL team penalty records for a final series were set. The record numbers were jacked up by a third-period brawl in game four, which accounted for 152 penalty minutes. A record 80 minutes went to the Canadiens and another record 25 minutes went to Claude Lemieux, who was assessed one minor, one major, one misconduct and one game misconduct.

The 1986 Calgary–Montreal Penalty Parade

Minutes	Finals Record
511	Most penalty minutes, both teams, one series
256	Most penalty minutes, one team, one series
176	Most penalty minutes, both teams, one game
152	Most penalty minutes, both teams, one period
90	Most penalty minutes, one team, one game
80	Most penalty minutes, one team, one period

9.15 **C. They hired a famous singer to belt out "God Bless America"**

Live or on tape, Kate Smith's version of "God Bless America" has a remarkable win–loss record for the Flyers at the Spectrum in Philadelphia. To gain the edge during game six of the 1974 finals against Boston, the Flyers flew Smith in for the real thing. Smith, an avid Flyers supporter ("I really do love those Flyers!") belted out the patriotic anthem (for $5,000 instead of her usual $25,000) and Philly became the first expansion team to win the Cup.

9.16 **C. Five players**

As of 1996, five NHLers have won playoff MVP honours twice: Bobby Orr (1970, 1972), Bernie Parent (1974, 1975), Wayne Gretzky (1985, 1988), Mario Lemieux (1991, 1992) and Patrick Roy (1986, 1993).

9.17 **A. None**

Maybe it was bad luck, shooter's nerves or just great goaltending, but none of the seven skaters awarded penalty shots during Stanley Cup final games succeeded in scoring. In fact, five out of seven times the shooter's team lost the game.

Penalty Shots in Cup Finals

Year	Shooter	Goalie	Final Score
1937	Alex Shibicky	Earl Robertson	NYR 0–Det 3
1944	Virgil Johnson	Bill Durnan	Chi 4–Mtl 5
1971	Frank Mahovlich	Tony Esposito	Chi 3–Mtl 4
1985	Ron Sutter	Grant Fuhr	Phi 3–Edm 5
1985	Dave Poulin	Grant Fuhr	Phi 3–Edm 8
1990	Petr Klima	Réjean Lemelin	Edm 7–Bos 2
1994	Pavel Bure	Mike Richter	NYR 4–Van 2

GAME 1: GOALIE GREATS

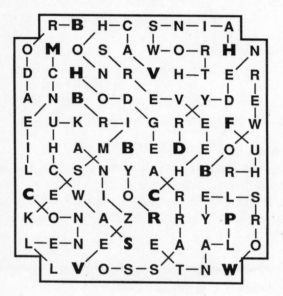

```
R—B H—C  S—N—I—A
O  M  O  S  A  W—O—R  H  N
D  C  H  N  R  V  H—T  E  R
A  N  B—O—D  E—V  Y—D  E
E  U—K  R—I  G  R  E  F  W
I  H  A  M  B  E  D  E  O  U
L  C  S  N  Y  A  H  B  R—H
C  E  W  I  O  C  R  E—L—S
K  O—N  A  Z  R  R  Y  P  R
L—E—N  E  S  E  A  A—L  O
L  V  O—S—S  T—N  W
```

GAME 2: NHL FIRSTS:
IN WHAT YEAR?

1. **1992**. The Pittsburgh Penguins won their second straight Cup on June 1, 1992, the first NHL game played in June.

2. **1937**. On April 15, 1937, referee Mickey Ion awarded Alex Shibicky the NHL's first penalty shot in finals history. Detroit's Earl Robertson stopped Shibicky's shot and the Red Wings won their second consecutive Stanley Cup.

3. **1971**. Bruins D-man Bobby Orr scored three playoff goals in a 5–2 win over Montreal on April 11, 1971. Since Orr's NHL first, eight other defensemen have equalled the mark.

4. **1934**. On April 10, 1934, the Hawks won their first Stanley Cup since joining the NHL in 1926. The victory came in a 1–0 overtime win over Detroit in game four on a goal by Harold March at 10:05 of the second OT period.

5. **1989**. Ron Hextall became the first goalie to register a playoff goal on April 11, 1989, during game five of the Patrick Division semifinal series against Washington.

6. **1959**. Since 1917, the only playoff season without at least one shutout occurred in 1959. Eighteen post-season games were played that year.

7. **1921**. The first NHL team to record back-to-back Cup victories were the 1920 and 1921 Senators.

8. **1945.** In the NHL's first rookie-versus-rookie netminder's duel in finals history, Frank McCool of the Leafs blanked the Red Wings and Harry Lumley 1–0 on April 6, 1945.

9. **1975.** Bernie Parent won his second consecutive Conn Smythe Trophy as playoff MVP when Philadelphia claimed its second-in-a-row Stanley Cup.

10. **1929.** On March 28, 1929, the Bruins and Rangers met in the NHL's first all-American finals. In the best-of-three series, Boston won 2–0 and 2–1 to claim its first Stanley Cup.

11. **1993.** On June 3, 1993, Montreal's Eric Desjardins potted the first hat trick by a D-man in a Stanley Cup finals game. His third goal was scored at 0:51 of overtime against Los Angeles.

12. **1950.** Left-winger Pete Babando's goal at 8:31 of the second overtime period on April 23, 1950, was the first Cup winner scored in game seven overtime in finals history. The 4–3 win over New York gave Detroit its first of four Cups in six seasons.

13. **1949.** After back-to-back Cups in 1947 and 1948, Toronto captured its third straight championship in 1949, a mark previously set 44 years earlier by the Ottawa Silver Seven in pre-NHL days.

14. **1969**. On May 4, 1969, Montreal's Serge Savard won playoff MVP honours, becoming the first NHL defenseman to win the Conn Smythe. A year later, Boston's Bobby Orr became the second MVP D-man.

15. **1941**. In only the third best-of-seven final series played since it was instituted in 1939, Boston routed Detroit 3–2, 2–1, 4–2, 3–1 for the NHL's first four-game sweep in 1941.

16. **1974**. In 1974, seven years after joining the NHL, the

Philadelphia Flyers became the first expansion team to capture the Stanley Cup.

17. **1940**. On March 19, 26 and 28 of 1940, the Rangers' Davey Kerr registered three shutouts in the Boston–New York semifinals, an NHL first in one playoff series.

18. **1948**. On April 7, 1948, 20-year-old Gordie Howe made his Stanley Cup debut in game one of the 1948 Detroit–Toronto finals. The Leafs swept the series four straight, and Howe failed to score.

19. **1995**. Dino Ciccarelli is tied with eight other NHLers for the most power play goals (three) in a playoff game. Only Ciccarelli, however, has done it twice: on April 29, 1993, and on May 11, 1995.

20. **1982**. On May 8, 1982, the Canucks became the first Vancouver team to play in the NHL finals since the WCHL's 1924 Maroons.

GAME 3: STANLEY CUP-WINNING GOALS

1. Mike Bossy
2. Uwe Krupp
3. Howie Morenz
4. Gordie Howe
5. Wayne Gretzky
6. Bobby Orr
7. Andy Bathgate
8. Mark Messier
9. Rick MacLeish
10. Baldy Northcott
11. Doug Gilmour
12. Ron Francis
13. Cy Denneny
14. Ab McDonald
15. Neal Broten
16. Ted Kennedy
17. Guy Lafleur
18. Craig Simpson
19. Bryan Hextall
20. Bob Nystrom

Q. The 1983 New York Islanders
D. The 1996 Colorado Avalanche
H. The 1930 Montreal Canadiens
T. The 1955 Detroit Red Wings
N. The 1988 Edmonton Oilers
B. The 1970 Boston Bruins
P. The 1964 Toronto Maple Leafs
L. The 1994 New York Rangers
M. The 1974 Philadelphia Flyers
J. The 1935 Montreal Maroons
G. The 1989 Calgary Flames
I. The 1992 Pittsburgh Penguins
S. The 1927 Ottawa Senators
C. The 1961 Chicago Blackhawks
O. The 1995 New Jersey Devils
R. The 1947 Toronto Maple Leafs
F. The 1976 Montreal Canadiens
A. The 1990 Edmonton Oilers
E. The 1940 New York Rangers
K. The 1980 New York Islanders

GAME 4: DEFUNCT TEAMS

1. L. Vancouver Millionaires
2. B. Kenora Thistles
3. Q. Quebec Bulldogs
4. J. Pittsburgh Pirates
5. O. Sydney Miners
6. I. Ottawa Silver Seven
7. K. Seattle Metropolitans
8. N. Victoria Cougars
9. C. Brandon Wheat Kings

10. F. Toronto Blueshirts
11. E. Portland Rosebuds
12. P. Edmonton Eskimos
13. H. Winnipeg Victorias
14. A. New York Americans
15. M. Calgary Tigers
16. G. Dawson City Nuggets
17. D. Montreal Maroons

GAME 5: THE HOCKEY CROSSWORD

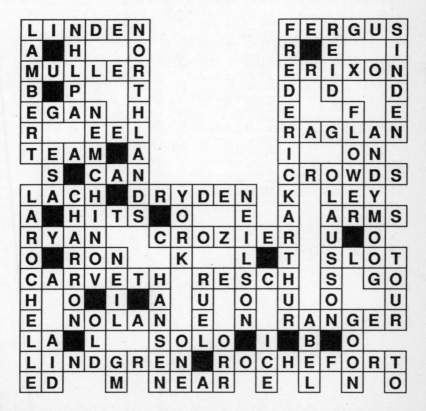

GAME 6: SEVENTH HEAVEN OR HELL

So whose goalie mask is in our sketch? Once all the words in the puzzle are circled and the remaining letters joined in descending order, it's revealed to be M-I-K-E R-I-C-H-T-E-R'S "Lady Liberty" mask.

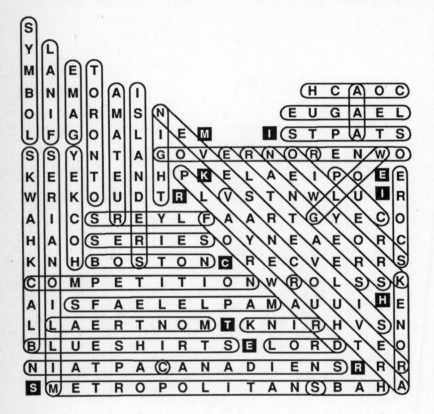

GAME 7: RECORDS OF THE CUP FINALS

1. Bernie Geoffrion
2. Brian Skrudland
3. Maurice Richard
4. Tony Esposito
5. Gordie Howe
6. Paul Coffey
7. Roy Conacher

8. Yvan Cournoyer
9. Ken Dryden
10. Larry Murphy
11. Jaromir Jagr
12. Mel Bridgman
13. Wayne Gretzky
14. Mike Bossy

15. Toe Blake
16. Bobby Orr
17. Jacques Plante
18. Jean Béliveau

GAME 8: THE PLAYOFF MVP

1. Jean Béliveau
2. Roger Crozier
3. Dave Keon
4. Glenn Hall
5. Ken Dryden
6. Bobby Orr
7. Bernie Parent

8. Reggie Leach
9. Bob Gainey
10. Butch Goring
11. Mike Bossy
12. Wayne Gretzky
13. Ron Hextall
14. Al McInnis

15. Bill Ranford
16. Mario Lemieux
17. Patrick Roy
18. Brian Leetch
19. Claude Lemieux
20. Joe Sakic

PHOTO CREDITS

Dan Diamond & Associates: page 6

Doug MacLellan/Hockey Hall of Fame archives: page 127

Bill Galloway/Hockey Hall of Fame archives: pages 73, 85

Graphic Artists/Hockey Hall of Fame archives: pages 38, 40

Hockey Hall of Fame archives: pages 10, 14, 22, 26, 29, 47, 48, 53, 57, 61, 76, 89, 95, 99, 109, 113, 114, 118

Imperial Oil–Turofsky/Hockey Hall of Fame archives: pages 17, 66, 123

Ray Lussier: page 131

Ville de Montreal/Hockey Hall of Fame archives: page 81

Western Canada Pictorial Index, University of Winnipeg/ Hockey Hall of Fame archives: page 71

ABOUT THE AUTHOR

Don Weekes is a television producer and writer with CFCF 12 in Montreal. He recently produced a 26-part short-feature series called *Hockey Legends* on the game's early years as well as the full-length documentary *Passing the Torch*, the story of the building of Molson Centre. This is his seventh hockey trivia book and his second in the *Old-Time Hockey Trivia* series.

ACKNOWLEDGEMENTS

The author gratefully acknowledges the help of Phil Pritchard and Craig Campbell at the Hockey Hall of Fame; Peter Schaivi, Holly Haimerl, Jim McCoy, Gerry Laderoute and Ross Francoeur at CFCF 12 in Montreal; the staff at the McLennan–Redpath Library of McGill University; Claire Lussier of Boston, Massachusetts; Robert Clements at Greystone Books; the many hockey writers and broadcasters who have made the game better through their own work; as well as my researcher Janet Torge, editors Kerry Banks and Anne Rose, fact checker Allen Bishop, graphic artist Ivor Tiltin and puzzle designer Adrian van Vlaardingen.